VICTOR FEATHER, TUC

Victor Feather, TUC

by

ERIC SILVER

LONDON
VICTOR GOLLANCZ LTD
1973

Hardback edition: ISBN 0 575 01359 1

Paperback edition: ISBN 0 575 01771 6

The cartoon by Les Gibbard on the title page "The Entertainer" appeared in the *Guardian* on 9 September 1970 and is reproduced by permission.

Printed in Great Britain by
The Camelot Press Ltd, London and Southampton

Contents

Illustrations

Acknowledgements

THE FIRST TIME I discussed this book with Victor
Feather he rejoiced that I had "the right mixture of
cynicism and idealism" for the task. I asked him to allow
me "scepticism". I hope he does so still. The job could
not have been done without its subject's undemanding
co-operation. He talked endlessly and with few reservations, but chose not to read my manuscript. I am grateful
to his family and to mine for their forbearance and
encouragement. Victor Feather's sister, Mrs Winifrid
Hayward, was a valued source of photographs and
information on the early years.

I was fortunate in being able to consult Feather's three
predecessors as general secretary of the Trades Union
Congress, Lord Citrine, Sir Vincent Tewson and George
Woodcock. My thanks to them and to their successors on
the general council and in the TUC secretariat. Two
of Feather's longest-serving colleagues—his secretary,
Jeanne Henbrey, and his chief information officer, Bob
Hartwell—deserve special mention. So does my former
partner in the *Guardian* Labour team, John Torode. All
three offered advice and corrections at every stage.

On the political side, I interviewed five of Harold
Wilson's Ministers. My gratitude to them in their anony-
mity. For material on the Bradford period I am indebted,
among others, to Mrs Alice Barber, James and Muriel

Nichol, and Aldermen A. A. Wallis and E. Newby. My first editor, Solly Pearce of the Leeds W*eekly Citizen*, provided a bridge between my part of the West Riding and Victor Feather's.

The following books are quoted with the kind permission either of publishers or of authors:

Socialism Over Sixty Years: The Life of Jowett of Bradford—by Fenner Brockway with a Preface by J. B. Priestley (Allen and Unwin for the National Labour Press).

Men and Work (Vol. 1) and *Two Careers* (Vol. 2): *The autobiography of Lord Citrine* (Hutchinson).

The Labour Government 1964–1970: A Personal Record—by Harold Wilson (Weidenfeld and Nicolson with Michael Joseph).

The Battle of Downing Street—by Peter Jenkins (Charles Knight).

Their Very Own and Golden City—by Arnold Wesker (Jonathan Cape).

E. S.

Prologue

THE BRITISH LABOUR movement is a common law marriage of working-class self-interest and Socialist idealism. It is not, however, simply a coalition of the big industrial battalions and the intellectuals of Holland Park. For most Labour activists, the impulse towards trade unionism and the impulse towards social democracy coincide. Both spring from the experience or perception of inequality, and the conviction that injustice and deprivation are not laws of nature. Long before he entered Winston Churchill's wartime Government, Ernest Bevin was a political as well as an industrial giant. Arthur Deakin and Bill Carron, who sustained party leaders, were no more a-political than Frank Cousins and Jack Jones, who challenged them. The unions have often embarrassed Labour Governments, but without them as an integral part of the same movement the parliamentary party would pack no more punch than the Liberals or the Co-operative Union. The working class, through the trade unions, is not just the paymaster of the Labour Party. It is the largest segment of its constituency, the key to its resilience and its power.

Victor Feather was a child of this Labour movement just as, in other circumstances, he might have been a child of the Roman Church or a son of the ghetto. The movement was his family, school and church, his club, his theatre and the channel for his ambition. He was born into it, and has never wanted to leave it. His Socialism was a constant, emotionally and intellectually. It was adaptable, but never demanding fundamental reappraisal. Socialism meant that people would no longer have to suffer the poverty and humiliation he had known in his youth. Socialism was an ethical as well as an economic concept. It meant freedom, self-respect and mutual responsibility. Communism was an authoritarian heresy.

The movement could easily have become a forcing house and Feather a narrow, parochial ideologue. Happily they did not. In Bradford, the birthplace and stronghold of the Independent Labour Party, it was people as well as institutions. The movement opened windows, stimulated palates and offered opportunities. The aspiring young could study at its classes, write for its newspaper, act in its plays, work in its campaigns and dream their careers.

Without this heritage, Victor Feather would probably never have risen to general secretary of the Trades Union Congress. Certainly, he would not have been the kind of general secretary who endeared himself to the viewing and listening public between 1969 and 1973. But it does not explain how and why he emerged from the cast of thousands in his generation who shared his background and experiences. To put the question in its most immediate form, why did Victor Feather become general secretary of the TUC while his two brothers and one sister led the same humble, private lives as their parents? His elder brother, Edwin, became a rural councillor in Derbyshire, but that was the only family competition. One brother was a craftsman at the better end of the motor industry, the other a driver. Victor's sister, Winifrid, kept a corner shop in Lincoln.

I once put the question to Feather himself. "I suppose I was the aggressive one," he answered. Aggression is indeed one element in his personality. Not truculence or an appetite for violence, but a willingness to accept a fight, to go into the ring for the things he believes in or recognises have to be done. There is, too, a streak of rudeness, even bullying, which comes out when Feather feels vulnerable or thinks that the weak are being exploited. I have seen him very angry with British Railways when he thought the board was rushing the drivers into accepting a reduction in the manning of trains. Again, his answer to a reporter who asked why the chairman of the TUC was missing from the platform at the biggest union rally since the war was blunt, monosyllabic and brooked no supplementaries.

But a native aggressiveness can only be part of the answer. His sister, keeper of the family album and folk-lore, extended it. "Victor," she said, "had more assertiveness, more drive than the rest of us. He was a born reformer. As a schoolboy, he always got through his lessons quickly. He was the leading spirit at home. I have always thought he had a big percentage of father's quixoticness and mother's practicality."

Quixoticness ought perhaps to be in quotation marks. I asked Winifrid what she meant. As an example, she said that her father, the unpaid branch secretary of his union, once negotiated a contract for a number of his members to polish the panelling in Bradford Town Hall. As soon as he had recruited the workers, he gave up his own share of the job. Another man needed it more, he told his wife. He had a big family to support. "What about your children? Don't you need the work?" she asked him. "Oh, I'll find something else," he replied.

Harry Feather, Victor's father, seems himself to have been a mixture of the practical and the "quixotic". The pencilled draft of a handbill he produced for the ILP in the early twenties illustrates both qualities:

"The promised 'land fit for heroes to live in' *has not* yet been fulfilled, nor never will be under our capitalistic system. On the contrary matters are getting worse and worse for the workers and millions of people find themselves in a worse position than in the time before we 'won the war', whilst a small section are doing very nicely on accumulated profits made during the war. Millions of money are being wasted abroad to satisfy whims of adventurers whom the workers have put into power.

"The Churchills, [Lloyd] Georges, Carsons and Smiths are in power by the vote of the workers and their votes are always cast to bolster the tottering capitalist system. Don't be satisfied with 'doles and test labour'.

"Come to our meetings and demand a right to some of the things you have helped to produce. 'Rise like lions after slumber in unvanquishable number, shake your chains to earth like dew, which in sleep had fallen on you, ye are many they are few.' (Shelley)

"Meetings will be held every Sunday at 11.15 a.m. top of North Wing. If wet 105a Otley Road."

Victor's practicality is his strength. He is suspicious of theorists, though by no means anti-intellectual. He has a logical and independent mind, and is not too proud to use the expertise of his more academic staff. When he is confronted with a crisis or a dispute, his first question is likely to be: "What are the real problems?" Then it is a matter of knowing and assessing the people involved, psychology and *realpolitik*. He is the kind of Northern working man who believes in insurance policies and never being in debt, a brother you can come to in moments of difficulty.

On the "quixotic" side, however, Feather is a man who will take risks. As a Home Guard volunteer during the Second World War, he chanced his life to save three neighbours from a blitzed shelter. During the campaign against the Communist leaders of the Electrical Trades Union, he put his career at hazard by writing anonymous articles for the press. At a more trivial level, he refuses to wear a seat belt when he is being driven down a motorway.

Feather will do things because they are fun or fascinating. As a young amateur journalist, he reviewed the music hall. As a junior TUC official, he preferred to buy an Epstein head rather than put his savings to "better use" on a second-hand car. As general secretary, he wanted to know about inconsequential people. He liked to encourage the young and gifted.

But what were the springs of Feather's assertiveness, his drive, his reforming zeal? One can only speculate. He was a second son, old enough to have been taken to public and union meetings by his father and to have absorbed something of their passions. Edwin, the eldest, was more self-effacing, though not without strength in personal matters. It is a common pattern in sizeable families. Victor, again, was young enough to have benefited from Bradford's extension of secondary schooling after the First World War. It gave him a measure of his own ability, but poverty denied him the chance to go on to university or train as a teacher. As a child, he was temporarily crippled by rheumatic fever. It is the kind of challenge to which you either succumb or respond by fighting, sometimes to the point of overkill. Victor fought back and won.

When Feather was elected general secretary of the TUC, a Fleet Street commentator paraded him as "the man in a hurry". He meant that Feather had only four years to make his mark before being forced to retire, but the label could as easily have been applied to his life as a whole. Feather was always ambitious, always busy, always seeking platforms. In his five years at Hanson Secondary School, his reports show that he never missed a single day (though he was occasionally late). He has remained the eternal revolving man, travelling, speaking, wheeling and dealing. Even when he had reached the top of the TUC there was no relaxing. Feather treated with Prime Ministers, but he was still eating more pie and pea suppers than anyone else in the business. Few who wanted to see him were turned away. Help was on tap—for the Newspaper Publishers' Association, or for the sick brother of an old friend who had been made redundant without adequate compensation.

Feather's industry has a compulsive quality. As one of his colleagues once put it, he is like a soldier whose aim is to win a posthumous VC. What makes Victor run? First, there is undoubtedly a strong sense of service. An interviewer asked him at the end of a Yorkshire Television profile what he would choose for his epitaph. His self-conscious reply was: "I would like to think—and this perhaps sounds a little bit trite—I think, that he tried to help."

In his early trade union days, as a shop collector at the Bradford Co-op, Feather was approached one day by the police to help a young woman workmate. Her illegitimate baby had died in suspicious circumstances. Feather did not see that it was either his or the union's business. When he told his mother the story over the tea table, she

Socialist Sunday School outing c. 1914–15.
Victor at front with cap. Father in back row right with moustache and trilby. At far left of second and third rows, Harry and Norah Feinburgh. Edwin Feather on Victor's left in front row.

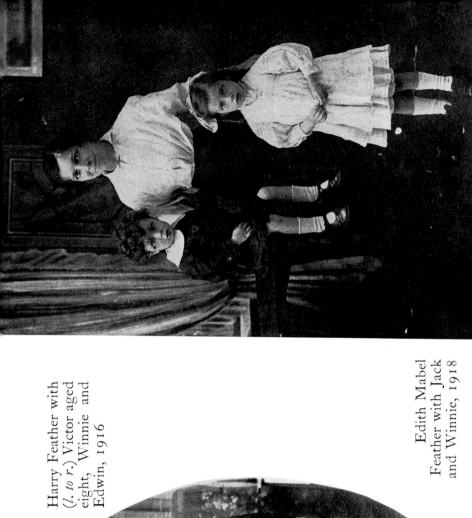

Harry Feather with (*l. to r.*) Victor aged eight, Winnie and Edwin, 1916

Edith Mabel Feather with Jack and Winnie, 1918

asked him what he was going to do about it. He said there
wasn't much he could do. His mother turned scornfully
on him and said: "I never thought I would live to be
ashamed of one of my lads." Victor took the next day off
work, borrowed the train fare to Manchester and insisted
on seeing the general secretary of his union. Eventually he
persuaded the union to help. The memory of his mother's
words stayed with him.

Feather's sense of service is matched by his sense of
community. His community is the trades councils, the
Labour clubs, the local chairmen and secretaries he knew
in his youth and has been paid to advise since he went to
the TUC in 1937. He is at ease among them, as he is
with journalists and broadcasters. They give him warmth
and assurance. They are an encouraging audience for the
Archie Rice in Vic Feather, the Entertainer who has to
go on earning his laughs. They fend off a suburban
alternative.

But above all, Feather is the supreme fixer. Among his
British contemporaries, perhaps only Lord Goodman is
in the same league. Like Goodman, Feather collects
people. Yorkshire Television judged him "a man without
friends—only an abundance of warm acquaintances". The
point is valid, but there is no cynicism in his relationships.
His memory for faces, names and events is phenomenal.
He remembers people, they remember him. They feel as
if they *are* his friends. They trust him, and he can turn to
them for help when he needs it. A difficult and damaging
strike? Who do we know there? A word on the telephone,
which Feather uses almost as assiduously as Lyndon
Johnson did. An awkward procedural dispute? Who do
we know on the board? A quiet meeting can be
arranged.

B

The rôle has its limits. The fixer can make it possible for his "clients" to achieve things. He can seldom guarantee that they will do so. Goodman could promote an agreement between Ian Smith and Alec Douglas-Home, but he could not promise that the Rhodesian settlement would stick. Feather could bring the newspaper publishers and the printing unions around the same trough, but he could not force them to drink.

Vanity is the fixer's final temptation. There were moments after 1969 when Feather seemed to think he could settle any of the world's conflicts, given the time and the opportunity. He did have at least one unpublicised success outside—though not without recourse to—his industrial beat. At the end of 1971 Britain and Malta had reached the end of a historic road. The Maltese Labour Prime Minister, Dom Mintoff, was demanding more money for the British base facilities. Lord Carrington, Edward Heath's Defence Secretary and chief negotiator, was refusing to pay another pound. The deadline was approaching. British troops would have to withdraw, Malta would face bankruptcy.

At this juncture, Feather had an anxious call from Bill Kendall, general secretary of the Civil and Public Services Association (the former Civil Service Clerical Association). The jobs of 300 of his members—Maltese civilians employed on the British base—were in danger. The opening was there. It was up to Feather.

First he telephoned his old friend, George Agius, general secretary of the Maltese General Workers' Union (the island's TUC). Please would Agius go and see *his* old friend, Dom Mintoff, and find out whether Whitehall really had heard his last demand. Agius went, then called back. Mintoff, he reported, was looking for a way off the hook. Informal contacts had already been made between the Foreign and Commonwealth Office and the TUC international department. Now it was time for Feather to call on another acquaintance, Denis Greenhill, Permanent Under-secretary and Head of the Diplomatic Service. He found that the Governments of Malta and the United Kingdom were no longer in touch.

Greenhill was interested, and encouraged Feather to pursue his private diplomacy. Feather spoke again to his Maltese counterpart. He asked him to discover what Mintoff's position now was. Agius was to dictate it over the telephone to the TUC as if it were his own message, though Feather would understand that it was actually Mintoff's. All went as planned, and Feather was able to signal back that although Britain's offer could not be increased, there might be more money forthcoming from NATO. Mintoff's ultimatum was waived. Talks were renewed four days later, though it was three months before a settlement was reached.

If Feather had less success with Ireland and the Israel–Arab conflict, it was not for want of trying. The instrument available to him, the trade unions, proved less responsive or less influential than he had hoped. As another quiet service to the Conservative Government Feather did, however, persuade the American dockers and airport workers not to black British cargoes. The boycott was threatened after "Bloody Sunday", 30 January 1972, when British paratroops shot dead 13 Ulster Catholics in Londonderry. Feather was already planning to attend the February meeting in Miami of the executive board of the American Federation of Labor-Congress of Industrial Organisations. He discussed the embargo privately with George Meany, the Czar of the American unions, with Teddy Gleason, of the International Long-shoremen's Association, which controls the East Coast ports, and with Matt Guinan, the airport men's Irish-American leader. Meany invited him to address the executive, where again Feather argued the case against blacking Britain. As a result of his efforts, the ban was limited to a token day.

The mission kept him away from the miners' strike for a couple of days longer than most commentators thought wise, but Edward Heath for one appreciated his reasons. On 22 February the Prime Minister wrote to the TUC general secretary from No. 10 Downing Street: "I have seen a report of your successful efforts at the AFL–CIO meeting to combat the proposal for a boycott of British goods. I wanted you to know how much this had been appreciated." In the Talleyrand tradition, neither Heath nor Feather sought public acknowledgement.

CHAPTER ONE

Socialism in one household

HARRY FEATHER WAS a Socialist of deep conviction and variegated taste. Having done his family duty by calling his firstborn Edwin, after his father, he named the other three children for the movement. His second son was called Victor Grayson Hardie Feather after two of the heroes of Labour's early parliamentary battles. His daughter was called Winifrid after the daughter of Robert Blatchford, the editor of the Socialist weekly *Clarion*. And his youngest was registered as Jack Hyndman Feather after H. M. Hyndman, leader of the Marxist Social Democratic Federation.

The future general secretary of the Trades Union Congress was born in Malvern Street, Bradford, on 10 April 1908, in circumstances that would have stretched the imagination of a Dickens. His father, a french polisher, was working out of town and came home about once a week. His mother had given what money she had to another woman to buy food for herself and Edwin, then six, while she was confined. The woman took the money, but never came back. The only food Mrs Feather had in the house was oatmeal. She and Edwin lived on "skilly", a thin gruel of oatmeal and water which she taught the boy to make. By this time, too, the baby had caught measles, from which Edwin was just recovering. When Harry Feather arrived home, he found them in desperate straits. He pawned his wife's wedding-ring to buy food for mother and children and new boots for himself.

Harry was one of the sappers of the Labour movement: a man who never stood for public office, but was the (unpaid) Bradford branch secretary of his union, an organiser of meetings for the Independent Labour Party, part-time agent in local elections, an adviser to conscientious objectors in the First World War. Victor remembers him as "a very determined man, not a very robust man, rather tall, rather thin-faced, a very prominent nose". Vincent Tewson, another Bradford man, who was general secretary of the TUC from 1946 to 1960, says he was "a tall, slim, dignified man, a pipe-smoker, walked very straight, a very, very clear thinker, one of the old pioneers".

Victor's mother was born Edith Mabel Bean. Her father was a chemist with a shop in the Hyde Park district of Leeds, and her grandfather had been a doctor. Both her parents had died by the time she was nine (when she met and married Harry they were both orphans), and Edith was fostered without much enthusiasm by an uncle and aunt. They sent her into domestic service when she was eleven, and she was working as a parlour maid for the Bradford mill-owning Illingworths when she met her husband. To her children, she was the great domestic manager, the practical counterpoint to Harry's idealism. Somehow, she kept them fed, clothed and housed through the years of low wages, irregular work and eventually disablement. "We had good food," Victor recalls. "Good food in the sense that it was cheap food. Perhaps we'd spend more on food nowadays and get less value. It was quite a thing to go for a pennyworth of marrow bones from the butcher's, and we used to get good soups, soups made of marrow bones and celery tops, carrots, turnips.

There was nothing fancy about it, dripping and bread. I think I was about twenty before I tasted butter regularly on my bread. We used to get dumplings. We'd stand at the table with a basinful of soup, perhaps about a pint of soup with a couple of pretty hefty dumplings in it. When I think back, I think the food I got then was about as tasteful as any of the food I get now." Alice Barber, whose husband Revis Barber was secretary of the Bradford Trades Council, remembers Edith Feather as "a small woman, kind, not very politically minded. She lived religion, though she was not religious in the ordinary sense. She once said to me, 'If ever Revis is taken ill, I'll come to be with you, no matter where I am.'" When Edith died in 1958, Alice Barber conducted the secular funeral service.

According to family legend, Harry Feather had wanted to call his second son Victor Grayson *Keir* Hardie Feather, but the registrar said there wasn't enough space. Victor Grayson and Keir Hardie both had national and local reputations. Hardie was a Scottish miner, who fought and won West Ham in 1892 to become the first independent Socialist MP. Four years later he contested Bradford East in a by-election, but came bottom of the poll. After the result was announced, Hardie told a meeting of supporters in the Peckover Institute of an old Scottish belief that in inspired moments certain people had a gift of second sight. His mother had been credited with this power. "I have a feeling that this gift is with me now," Hardie said, "and I am urged to make a prediction that Socialism will come in the year which bears the figures of my poll." Hardie's vote was 1953. F. W. Jowett, Bradford's first Labour MP and a Minister in Ramsay MacDonald's 1924 Cabinet, told the story in 1943 to his

biographer, Fenner Brockway. "There is yet time,"
Jowett added.

Victor Grayson presented a more persistent aura of
mystery. In Francis Williams's phrase, "He was of the
prophets and agitators." Grayson abandoned his theo-
logical studies in Manchester to fight a by-election in
Colne Valley as an unofficial Socialist in July 1907, and
astonished the party leadership by winning the West
Yorkshire seat. He quickly became one of the biggest
draws on the Northern Socialist circuit. "A young fellow
was on the chair, with a deep rich voice, just made for the
open air," the ILP *Labour Leader* reported of one of
Grayson's early meetings. "He was giving his audience
plain, strong, and richly-defined Socialism. Nothing petty
or mean, no appeal to unworthy motives, or even to the
misery of things, but an uplifting, elevating manly
propaganda speech, addressed to the crowd as men."

To the more austere Socialists like John Bruce Glasier,
however, Grayson was already suspect. When he was
rebuked for appearing in a dinner jacket at a Manchester
debate, Grayson retorted that he viewed with unspeakable
loathing the simple life, liked champagne and turtle
soup, and wished all the workers to enjoy them. He was
ambitious and, increasingly, an opportunist. On one
occasion, Jowett was sitting next to him in the Commons.
Grayson was anxious to raise some point. At 11 p.m.
Jowett nudged him and said, "Now's your chance to get
in, Victor." Grayson shook his head, pointed to the empty
press gallery and replied, "Look up there." He lost Colne
Valley in 1910, appeared in the bankruptcy court in 1914,
and went to Australia (and subsequently to New Zealand)
with his new wife at the end of the year. Grayson returned
to Europe with the New Zealand forces and was brought

back to England in 1917 after being wounded in the trenches. Little is known with any confidence of what happened to him after he left the military hospital. One day in 1920 he booked into a hotel in the Strand. He walked out, did not return, and was never positively identified again. His bag was sent to his family by the hotel manager, who said it had been left by a man with an injured arm and head.

The house where Victor Feather was born in Malvern Street, off Leeds Road, was typical of the long, cramped stone terraces built in the last century to shelter the workers drawn into the grey hills and valleys of Bradford by the woollen mills. It was a "small back-to-back", one room up, one down, with a windowless cellar, no through draught, and shared outside lavatories. Writing of the Bradford of a decade before Feather's birth, Jowett recorded: "Insanitary conditions and low wages made life difficult for working-class parents with young children. They looked forward expectantly to their children reaching working age, for the small weekly additions to the family income which they would bring into the home . . . Whilst children were under working age, food and clothing were insufficient. Yet going to work too early in life stunted growth, weakened constitutions, and therefore was a heavy price to pay for the few extra shillings a week."

Change came slowly and had to be won every inch of the way, with Councillor Jowett at the head of the reforming column. But by 1908, Bradford had made its mark as a centre of political and social innovation. The Bradford Trades Council sent a resolution to the TUC's Glasgow conference in November, 1892, declaring that the time had come to form a new party, independent and pledged to make the condition of labour the paramount question in British politics. Within three months, on 13 and 14 January 1893, the Independent Labour Party was born in the Labour Institute, Peckover Street, Bradford.

Socially, the city was a pioneer in public housing, child health and free secondary education. The first slum clearance project was started in 1901, with the tenants rehoused in corporation tenements. The first school meals in the country were served in the White Abbey dining rooms in 1907 (under the supervision of Jonathan Priestley, headmaster of Green Lane School, and father of J. B. Priestley). Less successfully, Bradford experimented too with the first municipal milk supply, pasteurised and bottled at a time when such hygienic refinements were rare. And it was in Bradford that Margaret McMillan, who had gone there as an ILP lecturer from London in 1893, began her campaign for child health. She was elected to the school board in 1894, and was soon demanding that the children should be as well looked after as the buildings. Bradford responded with swimming baths, fresh-air schools, and school clinics years before local councils were authorised by Act of Parliament to spend money on them. By the time Victor Feather was ready for secondary school, Bradford had abolished fee-paying and opened the doors to anyone who could pass the scholarship. In its hardheaded, businessman's way, however, the city waited until 1918 and an enabling Act before ending half-time working (children from the age of twelve spending half the day at school and half in the mill).

Then, as now, Bradford was a cluster of villages rather

than a single town. If you ask a Bradfordian where he comes from he is more likely to answer "Wyke" or "Wibsey", "Idle" or "Eccleshill", than "Bradford". But the place has always kept a corporate pride to fling in the eyes of outsiders. "In those pre-1914 days," J. B. Priestley writes in his preface to Jowett's biography, "Bradford was considered the most progressive place in the United Kingdom. . . . Our subscription concerts were famous; in addition we had our permanent symphony orchestra and two magnificent choral societies; and we had two theatres, besides the music halls and concert party pavilions; a flourishing arts club; and three daily papers . . . I am prepared to bet that Bradford produced more well-known people—musicians, scientists, writers, performers and the like—than any place anything like its size in the whole kingdom." 'Appen.

CHAPTER TWO

School and schooling

WHEN VICTOR FEATHER was six months old, the family moved to Gainsborough in Lincolnshire, where his father had found a job with a furniture company. Like Mary's little lamb, under-age Victor followed his brother Edwin to school. Unlike the lamb, he stayed till the family moved back to Bradford when he was five. Harry Feather had decided the wages were so poor that he would be better off at home. The Feathers found a house in Ripon Street, off the Otley Road. Again it was back-to-back, but not so small this time: two up, two down, with a sparrow-step of garden in the front. You still had to go out and down the passage to the lavatory, but it did have water and it wasn't shared. Ripon Street, where Victor lived till he was twenty-two, was built of grey-brown Yorkshire stone (plenty to be quarried locally and cheaper then than bricks). The long, straight road was paved in sets, oblongs of stone, bigger, flatter and more regular than cobbles. Half a mile to the south-west and down the hill, you could see the town centre, a sooty landscape of mills and offices. Soon the Feathers moved across the street to a house facing south—sixpence a week more on the rent, but worth it for a sight of the sun. Victor re-visited Ripon Street for a television documentary early in 1971. The houses stood empty and condemned. A year later, only the road and the rubble remained.

Harry Feather was quickly active again in the ILP and his union, the Amalgamated Furnishing Trades Association. Within a couple of years, young Victor was getting his first taste of the Labour movement. His father was branch secretary of the union, with about fifty or sixty members under his wing. They met on Sunday mornings in the Building Trades Hall in John Street, and when he was eight Victor started going there with him. First he was entrusted with entering the contributions in the branch book, graduating at ten to delivering sick pay.

Militancy often cost Harry his job. Employers would advertise for french polishers, but when they heard that Feather had applied they would suddenly discover that they didn't need any after all. Or they would engage him, then give him his cards when they spotted him organising the other workers. Jobs were scarce, and there was no need to employ "troublemakers". Father Feather fell back more and more on polishing coffins, single commissions for undertakers who wanted a couple finished in a hurry. Victor would often take him his sandwich lunch. He can, he says, still savour the smell of methylated spirits and wood shavings. "I had a fascination for seeing him at work, and seeing the other people there in the wood shop."

During the First World War, Victor was inducted in another form of dissent and its organisation. His father was a pacifist, though his health was probably too frail to have carried him through a medical. Harry was drafted into a munitions factory, Phoenix works in Bradford. Although it was a steady job with the prospect of good money, it conflicted with his principles. He used to work as little as he could, seldom bringing home more than £3 a week. He was often absent from work, preferring to give his time to a committee that helped conscientious objectors to marshal their case before the tribunal.

They came to the Feathers' house for advice or help. Sometimes they were on the run. Once or twice young Victor was taken to Malham, a desolate place at the source of the Aire, where ten or fifteen conscientious objectors had set up a communal market garden for themselves. "They were living out there," he says, "growing a bit of food, reading books and giving lectures to one another." Victor would also go with his father to put up the stump at open-air anti-war meetings that were often very tough.

He came uncomfortably close to death twice before he was ten. The first occasion was an accident when he was about five. He was reminded of it twenty-four years later when he went to work at the TUC. Vincent Tewson was the assistant general secretary, one of the men who had given him his job in the organisation department. Feather mentioned to Tewson, ten years his senior, that they had lived in the same district in Bradford. "We used to play on a wall at the top of your street. I once fell off it." Tewson says he peered at Feather and asked how old he had been when it happened. Victor answered that he must have been about five.

Tewson offered to tell him (and, more than thirty years later, me) a story: "You know the street. The wall was very high on our side of it. A road at a higher level runs across the top where the same wall is only three feet high, so boys could play about on it. One day I was talking to a lad at the top of the street, quite near that wall, when some boys came to play on it. We shooed them off. We didn't like people on our wall. They came back. We shooed them off again. Then finally we heard a cry. We looked round and saw that one of the boys had come back.

He'd fallen off the wall and was impaled on the railings, six feet below the wall. We ran there and lifted the boy off. He was very lucky, this boy, because the fellow I was with was not a hundred per cent, but he was a Scout and he knew first aid. He had the presence of mind to put his thumb in the wound in the boy's thigh where the railing had entered, and we carried him half a mile to a doctor."

Tewson asked Feather who his doctor had been. "Dr Parker," he replied. The pattern was complete. "I didn't know that the boy who had fallen many, many years before was Victor Feather," Tewson says, "and he didn't know that I was one of the two chaps who lifted him off."

Three or four years later, Victor contracted rheumatic fever. The same Dr Parker, a bluff, gentle, Scottish Socialist, told his mother there was nothing more he could do. He did not expect the child to live much longer. But Edith Feather, as her daughter puts it, was an instinctive nurse. In her later years, when she lived in Lincoln with Winifrid, she would often talk about her prescription and treatment.

The only thing, she had said, was a mustard bath. She put mats across the bottom of the door to keep out the draught, stoked the fire, and brought up the bath tub from the cellar. Victor was immersed in a steaming mustard bath. Suddenly he stiffened. "You've done it now," his father said. His mother lifted the boy from the bath and wrapped him in a blanket in front of the fire. About an hour later, beads of sweat began to form on his forehead. "Thank God," his mother sighed. Victor recovered, but the rheumatic fever left him with a weak valve in his heart. He was supposed never to swim or play games—an injunction he consistently ignored until well into his strenuous sixties, when he was still keeping wicket

for the TUC against the industrial correspondents, and
inaugurating swimming baths for union convalescent
homes at the drop of a snorkel. (The present writer was
once caught behind the stumps by Feather. The general
council's appeal could have been heard all the way from
Blackpool to Bloomsbury. When I protested that the ball
had hit my pad, the imperturbable umpire, another
Yorkshireman, John Newton of the Tailors and Garment
Workers, ruled that I was out either way: "If it hit your
bat, you were caught. If it hit your pad, you were LBW.")

Conventional religion had little or no place in the
Feather household. Harry Feather was as fiercely hostile
to the Roman Catholic Church as he was to Communism.
Victor was not baptised, but his mother named him in the
doorway of the Labour Church in Peckover Street (the
same building where the ILP was founded). Victor had
been an ailing baby, and a pair of old women neighbours
had told Edith Feather that he would never prosper until
he had been christened. So she took him to the Labour
Church, named him without ceremony or witness, and
carried him home. "I've done the right thing now," she
told her husband.

The Bradford Labour Church was another of Fred
Jowett's innovations. Liberal Non-Conformists staged a
meeting on 13 June 1892, in support of Alfred Illing-
worth, the sitting Liberal MP. They were worried by the
threat of Ben Tillett, the London dockers' leader, to stand
against him in Bradford West. The chairman said he was
at a loss to understand why the labouring classes should be
dissatisfied with the Liberal Party. Jowett intervened and
addressed the parsons on the platform: "If you persist in
opposing the Labour movement, there will soon be more
reason than ever to complain of the absence of working

Name	*Victor Feather*	Age	*15 yrs 3 mth*
Form	*5a*	Half-Year Ending	*July 31/13*
No. of Boys in Form	*22*	No. of Times Absent	*None*
No. of Times Late	*2*	Marks Possible in each Subject	*40*

SUBJECT	Marks obtain'd	REMARKS	Master's Initials
1 Mathematics	*34*	*Very good work done*	*aR*
2 English Lang. & Lit.	*35*		
3 Composition	*35*		
4 Reading & Recitation	*36*		*W.C*
5 Spelling & Writing	*34*		
6 History	*35*		*BJ*
7 Geography	*33*		
8 French	*32*		*Aug 8t.*
9 German	*34*		*39.*
10 Latin			
11 Chemistry	*34*		
12 Physics	*34*		*cW*
13 Art			
14 Music			
15 Shorthand & Typewriting			
16 Commercial Arithmetic			
17 Manual Work			
18 Homework		*Extremely well done*	*aR*
19 General Conduct & Manners		*Very good*	*aR*

Summary *The work of the half year deserves the highest praise. Excellent progress made.*

Parent's Signature

W.E.315—500

School report at the age of fifteen

East Bradford Socialist Sunday School leaving for May Day procession, late 1920s. Victor standing on far left of cart, above back of horse

men from your chapels. We shall establish our own
Labour church."

Jowett was true to his word, and the Labour Church
spread throughout the North of England, presenting
Socialism as an ethical gospel reinforced by Labour
hymns sung to the old chapel tunes. Its members believed
in God in the sense of God being Good. Victor Feather's
mother believed in some sort of creator, some divine
being. Her son is not sure that he has ever done so. "I
suppose, like lots of youngsters at that time, I claimed to
be an atheist. Later on, of course, I said I was an agnostic.
Later still, I wouldn't claim now to be either an atheist, or
an agnostic, or a Christian, or in that sense a religious
man."

What the young Victor had in place of Christ was the
Socialist Sunday school. The Sunday school was separate
from the Labour Church. It taught neither God nor
Christianity, but ethics. Half a century later, Feather can
still recite its message: "Make every day holy, they said,
by good and useful things. Not just one day holy, not a
Sunday or a holy day. Make every day holy by good and
useful deeds and kindly actions. They weren't limiting it.
Observe and think, in order to discover the truth. Do not
believe what is contrary to reason, and never deceive
yourself or others, So again, don't lie, you see, don't steal.
But then, of course, they took a broader view of stealing.
Remember that he who enjoys the good things of the
earth without working for them is stealing the bread of the
workers. These were some of the Ten Precepts. Another
one was do not think that those who love their own
country must hate and despise other nations, or wish for
war, which is a remnant of barbarism."

The Sunday schools were not just for children. The

c

classes ranged from "baby" to "adult". Older members
would be both pupils and teachers. One of Feather's
teachers was Norah Feinburgh. One of his pupils was her
son Wilfred, the future Labour MP and novelist. Children
brought to the Sunday school were dedicated to humanity,
and to working for the improvement of humanity. The
schools, which had no financial backing, rented classrooms
from the local education authority, or borrowed Labour
halls. From time to time, they were attacked in the press
as "Red nurseries of atheism", and the council schools
would be closed to them. "We used to meet at one time
for about twelve months over some stables," Feather
recalls. "The floorboards weren't very well jointed, and
the stench of the horse manure on a hot Sunday afternoon
was nobody's business."

Feather first went to the Socialist Sunday school when
he was six. In Gainsborough the family had been Unitar-
ians (the local Unitarian minister was a Socialist, and they
seem to have gone as much out of solidarity as conviction).
Victor continued as an active member of the Socialist
Sunday school into his mid-twenties. He dipped, too,
into the Quaker educational movement and the Co-op
Guild.

For his more formal Bradford education, Feather
graduated at ten-plus from Undercliffe elementary school
to Hanson secondary. Ahead of its time, the city had
abolished fee paying, and all of Victor's year were scholarship boys. Hanson had been built in 1903: a tall, stone
pile blending with the surrounding terraces, a class up on
Ripon Street, though within walking distance. It had
high ceilings; squared windows; and ninety-six steps,
slenderly railinged in wrought iron, from the entrance to
the main classroom corridor. The wooden huts, erected

in the playground as overspill classrooms during the First World War, are still there in the seventies. Hanson, housing separate boys' and girls' schools in Feather's day, has always had space problems. They were usually solved by creating more classrooms, rather than letting numbers rise above forty to a class. This sometimes meant partitioning rooms, so that one half finished with all the daylight and the other with all the heating. Hanson was known for its good workshops and its laboratories. One of the school's first pupils was Edward Appleton, who went on to a Cambridge chair, a Nobel physics prize, and his own Layer in the upper atmosphere.

Feather inherited his Hanson cap from Albert Wallis, who later became a Bradford alderman and an official of the Electrical Trades Union. Although in his Undercliffe years Feather had sometimes qualified for free school breakfasts as well as free school dinners, he was not quite among the poorest of Hanson boys. "One or two of the laddies wore clogs," he remembers. "Now this was a sign that you were on your uppers, if you wore clogs to school. We never wore clogs, but on the other hand the soles of our shoes weren't so thick either. But I suppose most of us wore shoes that had never been bought new for us. They were from jumble sales. And when the soles wore through —not only the first sole, but the second and the third one —you got quite adept at making cardboard inner soles to stick on. And when your got your feet wet, you just got your feet wet, and nobody was really concerned about it. I would hardly know a time when it really rained when I wouldn't get my feet wet, sometimes with a kind of bubble coming out of the welts of the shoes."

At Hanson, Feather enjoyed languages, surprised himself by doing well in mathematics, and won a second eleven cap for cricket. "He was a frank, even-tempered, sociable boy with light blue eyes, rather good at handicraft," his old English master, William Cox, confided to the *Yorkshire Evening Post* in June 1969. "He was not specially brilliant, but intelligent enough to take his School Certificate a year early." It was perhaps as well, for Feather could hardly have stayed at school much longer.

CHAPTER THREE

A stroke in the family

ONE SUNDAY EVENING, when Victor was fourteen, Harry Feather was sitting at the table in Ripon Street writing a postcard to F. W. Jowett, who was treasurer of the ILP. There had been an open-air meeting at the top of North Wing, and Harry was reporting on the collection (four or five shillings, subscribed in halfpennies). Victor had just gone to bed at about nine o'clock. "I was in bed in my shirt," he says. "Very few people in our circle at that time even knew what pyjamas looked like, never mind could spell the word or buy them." Suddenly, his mother called frantically: "Victor, Victor, come at once!"

He sprang out of bed because of the panic and urgency in her voice. "I nearly fell down the stairs into the room and saw my father there with his face twisted, lurching over the table with the green cloth on. I pulled him into a more upright position, and my mother said 'Run for the doctor quick. I'll manage your dad.' And I went upstairs and pulled on a pair of trousers. I remember I didn't bother with socks or shoes. I hurtled out of the door, and I suppose that to Dr Parker's from 223 Ripon Street was a good three-quarters of a mile, and I guess I did it in three minutes anyway. I rang the bell and kept on ringing the bell, and told the doctor he'd got to come at once."

The doctor came immediately and diagnosed a stroke.

Harry Feather, who was forty-two, fought hard. After a spell in St Luke's Hospital, he managed to get back his speech. His brain remained quick and clear. His daughter remembers him going through the daily papers from end to end. "He often wrote letters to them on political and trade union matters about which he felt deeply. I can remember, too, how he and Victor would have many arguments (and disagreements) about politics." But in spite of "fresh-air treatment", six-mile rides on a tram with the door wide open, Harry never recovered the use of his left arm. He had to walk with a stick, dragging his left leg, and was never able to work again.

Eventually, after five years, he told Victor that the doctors were misleading him. "I'm not going to get better, I know I'm not going to get better." And he refused his food. Victor bullied his sister, who was father's favourite, to make him eat. But it was no use. Harry Feather died on 7 April 1927, as much from starvation as from the effects of his stroke. He was forty-seven.

When his father was taken ill, Edwin Feather was twenty and on the point of setting up house on his own. By the time Harry died, Edwin was married and living out of Bradford. As the second son, Victor gradually assumed the man's rôle in the household. He left Hanson as soon as he had taken his School Certificate, at fifteen. It meant the end of his "official" education, a disappointment for himself and his parents, who had hoped he would go on to be a teacher. Fifty years on, Feather tends to laugh off his missed university education. "They give you the degree in the end" (Bradford University made him an honorary Doctor of Technology in December 1970). Or, "I might have had a chair of industrial relations". In 1923, though, it mattered. Hanson had spiced his palate without serving the full menu.

Her husband's illness tested Edith Feather's ingenuity and resilience more than ever. She would leave home at five in the morning to scrub wool merchants' offices in the middle of Bradford for, perhaps, 2*s* 6*d* a week. She had woken the children before she went, and Victor would see they had their breakfast. In the evenings, after the younger ones were fed and in bed, she sewed cheap shopping bags, made of American leather (linen backing with a shiny black front). This was out-work. A firm paid Mrs Feather a penny for four, stitched from ten to as late as one in the morning, and sold them for fourpence or fivepence each.

Victor was already contributing his small share to the Feather budget. He earned his first pay as a butcher's errand boy, delivering joints on Saturday mornings. It was worth two shillings (and now and again half a pound of sausages) for a long morning, starting at half-past seven and going on till half-past one. He was eleven or twelve, still below the legal minimum age for taking a job. Victor had also done a little fire-lighting for Jews, who could not kindle on the Sabbath. He would go by tram to Leeds, warm the hearths of half a dozen families in the Camp Road district, and charge them a penny a time. Since the tram fare was only a penny, and he could combine it with a visit to his Aunt Annie Bean, the trip was worth it.

Later, while still at Hanson, Victor was selected for the second eleven and needed his Saturday mornings for cricket. Instead, he found work for Saturday afternoons—his first contact with journalism. Young Feather would line up on a Thursday night outside one of Bradford's two evening paper offices—the *Telegraph* or the *Argus*—asking for a "sheet". If they didn't have a sheet, please could he be a "runner"? A sheeter wrote up minor-league matches for the Saturday sports editions. A runner presented himself to the staff reporter covering more important fixtures, and delivered his copy in relays to the office for quick printing. A sheeter earned 1*s* 6*d*, a runner 6*d*; but like all the best newspaper jobs, there were expenses too.

"If you were a runner," Feather reminisces, "you didn't telephone the copy, you jumped on a tram. We got very adept at riding the step. The journey was about a penny, and you were allowed the penny by the newspaper, but what was the point of having expenses if you couldn't make something out of them? So, we used to run alongside the tram and hope the conductor was upstairs or he was deep inside the tram. Then you could leap on the running board and crouch down and perhaps ride for 50 yards, 100 yards, 200 yards. You were hoping and praying, and you got very expert at leaping off, just as his arm was reaching out to take you by the shoulder to clout you, and running alongside then as fast as you could go and boarding the next tram as it overtook you.

"The sheeter was better because that meant you took full control. You were responsible not only for reporting the match, but also for delivering the stuff to the office. The referee once sent off both teams. There was a real punch-up, and my account was good enough to be not only a report of the football match, but it was a brilliant boxing report too. I got about four inches, but I didn't get paid any more for it. I might just as well have said who'd scored the goals. But you got more on expenses for being a sheeter. These matches were further out, on the outskirts of Bradford. So you would get twopence to get there and twopence to get back. And since you got there for nothing, because you set off in good time and were prepared to walk, that was twopence before you started. Then, coming back, if you could ride the trams on the running board, you made another twopence. But you'd got to be a bit careful because you couldn't get back too late with the report. You could never make it back to the office and save twopence, but you could always save a penny. You always had to have the last penny on a tram because you were working behind the clock."

Like his father, young Victor handed over his pay (expenses and all) to his mother, who would give him back a penny or two. The boy became skilled, too, at "saving a bit on the shopping". With some of his friends, he would go around the markets asking for bruised oranges, making sure there were some by bruising them first while the stallholder was looking the other way. Or they would "whip" a couple of extra apples or potatoes, even a slice of fish. "If it had been today," Feather muses with the authority of a CBE and the best office in Congress House, "I suppose we'd have been juvenile delinquents. We'd have been up in court, but then we used to get clouted by a policeman or a stallholder. We never pinched anything very big, but over a period we pinched plenty. My mother would have been horror-stricken if she had known. We persuaded her that we were the best shoppers in the business." His parents did find him out once, however. Young Victor was tempted by a cream horn in a baker's shop. The owner reported him to his headmaster, who gave him six of the best on each hand. His parents wanted to know why his hands were swollen, and when they had winkled the truth out of him, his father beat him with a leather strap.

Even before Harry Feather's stroke, it had been hard for his wife to make ends meet. Afterwards, she had to go for a supplement to the Board of Guardians. Sickness benefit was 15s 6d for a man and wife, plus 2s for each child, which gave the Feathers 21s 6d. But after a few months the sickness money was replaced by disablement benefit, which was only 10s 6d a week. So, Mrs Feather had to go every week to the Board of Guardians to collect another 8 or 10 shillings. One week she came back in evident distress. She was a pretty woman, and one of the relieving officers had made some kind of pass at her. Victor, aged fourteen, was outraged.

"I went down, and there was a very big queue outside the Guardians, perhaps about fifty people. I got half a brick, and I peeped through the Guardians' window, and I saw this huge crowd there and debated with myself. Then I let fly with the half-brick, and it went straight through the window. I'd intended to make some sort of public outcry. I wanted, I think, when I went down, to do this demonstration, then to face up to whatever consequences came—including, perhaps, being taken to the police and having to tell a magistrate why I'd done it.

"I let fly with the brick, and the brick went through the window all right, and there was a great gasp of pleasure from the people who were waiting. And then they saw me standing, and I remember quite vividly a woman who I thought at that time would be an old woman, because remember I was only fourteen, and perhaps she wasn't an old woman at all, perhaps she was only a woman of forty. And she said: 'Run, you silly little bugger, run!' And I suppose this galvanised me into action. Automatically, I ran like the wind. And if anybody wants to know who broke that window all those fifty years ago, that was me."

CHAPTER FOUR

Apprentice into journeyman

VICTOR FEATHER'S FIRST fifteen years had taught him
about poverty and self-respect, anger and resistance. You
didn't have to accept your lot. You could fight back. The
ILP, the Socialist Sunday school and the Co-operative
junior guild supplied the theoretical framework: an
English Socialism that took its principles from the
Non-Conformist Church and its passion from Marx.
Hanson school had given Feather a measure of his own
potentiality. He had won his scholarship; won his place
in the special class of twenty-two boys who were crammed
to take matriculation a year early; and won his School
Certificate with a distinction in mathematics. The two
Vics—the "practical" and the "quixotic"—were already
discernible. The next fourteen Bradford years, from
leaving school to joining the staff of the TUC, completed
the transition from apprentice into journeyman.

Feather said goodbye to Hanson on the Friday night
and started work on the Monday morning. Not everyone
found jobs so easily in 1923, but the Bradford Co-op
probably gave him preferential treatment. Harry Feather
was well-known as a Co-operator, Victor had attended its
guilds and its schools. The Labour men on the Co-op
board knew his father was ill, that Victor would become
the breadwinner. Like Walter Citrine, another future
general secretary of the TUC, Feather began his working

life as a flour boy. He filled and weighed sacks of flour for the Co-op at Girlington, earning 12*s* 6*d* a week, which had to be declared to the Board of Guardians, complete with humiliating signature from the Co-op manager. After about twelve months, he blossomed into a counter-hand, and eventually into second counter-hand (real promotion in a store employing about a dozen staff), and assistant manager. Although Feather always had ambitions to get out of the Co-op, he took his shopkeeping seriously. He went to night school and passed examinations for Membership of the Grocers' Institute. If he had to spend his life in grocery, he'd be sure of getting to the top.

Feather had his first taste of electioneering in 1918 as a ten-year-old, helping in Willie Leach's main committee room. By the age of fourteen or fifteen, he was regularly attending political meetings. At nineteen, he was an election agent in the East Ward of Bradford. For one local election, Feather recruited youngsters from the secondary schools. They were better writers than their mothers and fathers, and most of the leaflets were hand-written (printing cost money). All the administrative work was done by the children, aged anything from thirteen to fifteen, while the adults were sent to canvass on the door-steps.

Bradford ILP had a big children's choir, who marched and sang around the streets of the city and at party meetings. Feather took the idea a step further. They were getting poor attendances at municipal election meetings, down sometimes to ten or twenty on a wet night. What was needed, said the young agent-impresario, was a spot of light relief. The choir were dressed up as pierrots and renamed the Sunshine Follies. The meetings concentrated on a concert rather than too many speeches. "I was getting audiences of 80, 100, 120," Feather recalls with a touch of showbiz hyperbole. "About an hour and a half by the Sunshine Follies, about ten minutes by the candidate, and everyone went home very happy and voted Labour."

The first time Feather spoke in public was on Woodhouse Moor, a flat and gritty patch of common land about a mile from the centre of Leeds. He was fifteen, and argued the Darwinian case with a soapbox theologian. A year later, Feather heckled a speaker from the Economic League at an open-air meeting in Bradford. The speaker sneered and asked his young critic whether he would like the rostrum. Feather retorted, "Yes please," and the Economic League withdrew the offer. So Feather set up shop on a wall about fifty yards away, near the Bradford Northern Rugby League ground, and invited everyone to come and listen to him. Most of them did.

His duck was broken, and Feather soon became a regular attraction at the ILP's Sunday-morning street-corner meetings, catching the curious on the way home from church or the way out to the pub. Feather would stand on a borrowed chair and talk for five or ten minutes before introducing the main speaker. An audience had been gathered and warmed up. Feather took the chair more than once for Wilf Heywood, who later became general secretary of the Textile Workers and a member of the TUC general council. He learned, too, by watching such Sunday stars as Jowett and Leach, Willie Hirst and Norman Angel, who swept the board in Bradford in the 1929 general election. Then there was Alderman Meggison, who is remembered for having a voice like a megaphone.

Labour men who heard Feather playing the juvenile

lead testify that he was an energetic, entertaining orator who could hold a meeting before he was twenty. He was essentially a propagandist, rather than a speaker with original ideas. Feather arrived at one meeting to find his name writ large as principal speaker. He sat modestly in the front row, leaving the stage to the chairman and supporting cast. All went well until the chairman leaned over and whispered anxiously: "What time's your father coming, lad?"

Besides watching and imitating, Feather took night-school lessons in elocution from an ex-actor called Price. He learned public speaking, too, at classes run by the National Council of Labour Colleges (where he also studied economics) and the ILP. Half a dozen aspiring MacDonalds would go out to the moors and practise orating at each other. Then the ILP expert would show them how it ought to be done. Any actions must be above, or level with, the shoulder. Never speak with your hands in your pockets. Never fiddle with buttons (it only makes the audience nervous). Write your notes three words to the line, three lines together. Imagine you're talking to 1,000 people.

Feather learned another golden rule the hard way. One day in Shipley Glen he was asking his (happily non-existent) audience a rhetorical question. A couple of sheep poked their heads round a rock and answered: "Baaa, baaa." On another occasion, Feather was sharing a platform at Armley with John McGovern, the rebellious Scottish Labour MP. The chairman asked McGovern to speak up. "Can you hear me at the back?" McGovern bellowed. "No," a voice replied, "but it's all right."

Half the battle in open-air meetings was to entice your audience. There was no public address equipment, so you exaggerated your actions to catch the eye of people fifty yards away. Let's see what that fellow's waving his arms about, what that chap's jumping about for. But it was tiring work, and Feather soon devised his own alternative. He had already done some amateur cartooning. What better, in the cause of audience and productivity, than a bit of lightning caricaturing? It worked on the music hall, so why not on the street corner? Instead of setting up the stump, Feather set up an easel and sketched with coloured chalks on rolls of cheap wallpaper. His subjects were politicians—Baldwin, Chamberlain, Lloyd George, Ramsay MacDonald, Snowden—and while he was drawing the figures he was talking about their policies. The orator gave way to the entertainer, but the object was unchanged.

At about the same time, his late teens and early twenties, Feather edged into journalism. His mentor and patron was Frank Betts, a scholarly and (by Bradford standards) bohemian tax inspector, who was the father of Barbara Castle and edited the local Labour weekly, the *Bradford Pioneer*. Betts did not teach Feather his Socialism but he taught him to write and he opened windows. On the evidence of his own literary essays, published weekly for the best part of a decade in the *Pioneer*, Betts was not only a man of perception and taste but an inspired educator. He informed, analysed and stimulated, but without talking down to his readers. Feather was one of a handful of the gifted Labour young whom Betts invited to his house in middle-class Manningham Lane. The others included Horace Green, who became an organiser for the Communist Party in the North-East, and Mary Hepworth, who wrote fiction but never realised Betts's hopes for her as a novelist. The group met informally once a fortnight, sometimes once a month, and would discuss the world and its books from seven to ten or eleven at night.

Betts was regarded in Bradford as an eccentric. His priorities were "books, beer and baccy". Jim Nichol, who preceded him as editor of the *Pioneer*, describes Betts as "a tall fellow, not athletic, very wrinkled, with a greyish face, rather saturnine, and dark hair". His clothes were careless and unusually casual for a civil servant. Sports coats were not much worn in those days. And he always seemed to have a great woollen muffler. He was always going to catch a cold, or not catch one.

For Feather, Betts was an exotic figure. "I suppose his hair was longer than some of the hippies' hair today. But that was simply because he didn't have time to get his hair cut. I remember he was in that sort of class that had an annual subscription to the hairdresser. He could go as many times as he wanted. I should think it was the most lucrative payment that the hairdresser got because he didn't seem to go more than twice a year. I was with him once—this was a very pukka hairdresser that all the wool merchants used—and Frank Betts poked his nose round the corner and saw that the place was busy. He was about three months overdue for a haircut then, but he said to the hairdresser, 'Oh, that's all right, you're busy. I'll come back when I come back from my holidays.' He was going abroad for a month, so I think the hairdresser had the best of that bargain by a long way."

In the early 1920s, Bradford was starved of drama. Priestley's theatres had gone over to the cinema. Betts was one of those who filled the gap as first producer of the ILP Arts Guild. His opening production was Galsworthy's *Strife*. Muriel Nichol, who was MP for Bradford North

Vic Feather with Walter Citrine, at his first congress after joining
the TUC: Norwich 1937

Vic Feather in 1942 at a time when he was giving a series of talks in the BBC Shortwave Service to the West Indies on the birth, growth and development of trades unionism in Britain from 1945 to 1950, played Maggie, the strike leader's wife. Betts, she says, was a very original producer, but merciless on his cast. He could tread on your toes one minute, then be all smiles the next. His wife, Barbara Castle's mother, once produced a pantomime in which Feather had a part. Betts, who spent ten years in Bradford, must have been very good at his job. Tax inspectors were not expected to involve themselves in politics. Yet the limit of his discretion was to write under his initials rather than his full name in the *Pioneer*, and to steer clear of the more conspicuous public platforms.

As a cartoonist, Feather would probably never have been more than a gifted amateur. A drawing for his union journal, a sketch for a Co-op advertisement, were about the right level, though this didn't stop William Davis commissioning a *Punch* cover from him in May 1972. His Bradford journalism is of a different calibre. Feather's articles, published under a quiver of by-lines in the *Pioneer* from 1927 till he left for London ten years later, display many of the qualities of a front-rank professional in embryo. He had a talent for observing the significant detail; an eagerness to find things out for himself; and the capacity to write fluently—often arrestingly—in a variety of personal styles. The amateur shows through in the bumptiousness of his satirical offerings, but a good Fleet Street sub-editor would soon have deflated that.

The only surviving set of bound *Pioneers* is kept in Bradford Central Library. The first Feather article I found in a day's search appeared on 4 March 1927, when he was not quite nineteen. It was signed "V. Eff" and was a knock-about column contrasting Sir Samuel and Lady Hoare's troubles with Channel fog (their flight was cancelled, and they had to complete the trip home from India by boat and train) with the crush on the Bowling Tide train home from Blackpool. It was addressed to a mythical Simple Simon called Reuben, and ended with the eternal punchline: "Scripes kid." Another piece, a fortnight later, was an attack on Eugene Ramsden, the Conservative MP for Bradford North, who had presented himself in the *Leeds Mercury* as "an authority on foreign affairs". It is worth preserving in aspic for the line: "Hello, Russia! I'm part of the export from the Land of Dope and Tory. Kiss me."

By April, "V. Eff" was writing in a different tone. His *For King and Country* was angry and pained:

"This week, for the first time in my life, I noticed at close quarters a funeral. . . . It was the funeral of a neighbour—a neighbour who had lived in Hell for the last nine years—a neighbour mentally and physically wrecked by the Bloody Shambles of 1914–18—a living contradiction of the sturdy pugnacious individual who is reputed to be British Manhood—John Bull!

"Five years ago my neighbour trod the streets of Bradford, head bowed and inclined to one side—every step a tremendous effort; poorly clothed with a despairing attempt at fashionable respectability. Face haggard and drawn: he didn't live, he existed.

"Four years ago they took him to hospital, and after a sojourn there of two years he was pronounced incurable. A human derelict—incurable! What pleasure could life offer to one who was incurable? He stayed at home six months, and then was again sent to hospital—this time a mental hospital. He died last week.

"During the whole of the period—1918–27, his wife had to apply to the Guardians for inadequate maintenance, and his wife, with five children, the eldest of whom is now seventeen and the youngest eight, has also existed, yet not lived; and her existence has been a worse Hell than her husband's for she has had to notice the things that her children lacked—her husband couldn't. . . .

"Nine years has she suffered—nine years has he died. He fought so that she may be happy—he fought because the parson, his employer, the politician, told him that he must if the world was to be safe for democracy.

"He doubted them not! He went—and returned, and the parson can still take his living from the people whom he persuaded to ruin themselves.

"That has been their mode of life for nine years, and when he was buried—a civilian funeral—the coffin bore a Union Jack, placed there by his widow—to show, as she said, 'Her loyalty.'"

This article appeared in the *Pioneer* dated 8 April 1927. Feather's pacifist father died on 7 April.

Later "V. Eff" took to reviewing concerts in the Jowett Hall, "packed to its utmost capacity" for Casey and Dolly (he of the talking fiddle, she a fine pianist) or for a "well-known elocutionist". As "Grayson", Feather began writing sketches of ILP meetings in 1929, and as "Bimbo" he was given a regular, provocative column, *Pen Scratches*, in July 1931. "Bimbo" was fanfared with a warning from the editor: "In introducing 'Bimbo' to our readers, we must warn them that he must not be taken too seriously, or our Correspondence columns will be choked. Amidst his humour and satire he has a message. You are to seek it as a change from crosswords. No prizes are offered." The columns began with a skit on economists, the Great Eat-Less-Bread Campaign, followed a fortnight later by the Great Grass-Eating Crusade. But before the nation had taken to the meadows, Ramsay MacDonald formed his National Government and the *Bradford Pioneer* seems to have lost its appetite for humour and satire.

In a moment of party crisis, Feather was nudged aside by the big guns (though the first Labour conference after MacDonald's defection was reported by young Barbara Betts, on vacation from Oxford). Feather was left to report election meetings, and write a post mortem calling over three columns for better propaganda, organisation and planning.

The most ecstatic of Feather's meeting reports had appeared during the 1929 election campaign. "Grayson" dilated over two and a half columns on *The Man of the Morrow: MacDonald at the Olympia*. The piece ended on the unhappy coda:

"He makes his audience think—they do not need to be made to shout. I felt that I was helping him—that we were solving a set problem together—felt that when we had finished we would jump up, clasp one another's hand, and say: 'The job's done! We know the answer. Let us both go out and tell everybody else!'"

But the best of Feather's *Pioneer* writing was his social reportage, sometimes fictionalised, sometimes hard and detailed. In July 1927, he wrote a first-person account of house-hunting in a poor district:

"Children played over the street sinks, from which came some of the typical stenches of the slums; children half-naked, or children so well garbed that their elder brother's trousers extended almost to the ankle. All were shoeless and stockingless; some were bonny, and some seemed so weak that it was a wonder that they could even play. One thing they all had in common, each and every one—from a wee mite of four (he *looked* about two years old) to the boss of the gang—knew what vocation Steve Donoghue followed. . . ."

Five years later, in March 1933, "Grayson" spent a night among the down-and-outs of Leeds:

"A bitterly cold night, with 10 degrees of frost; but underfoot it was dry, which was a consolation, for my shoes had thin soles and the heels were down to the uppers. Old grey flannel pants and a greasy cap, an ancient sports coat, dingy and patched, dirty khaki shirt, a crumpled tie, and a rubber mackintosh that keeps out the rain and lets in the cold, woollen socks, pullover, and vest, and an extra shirt comprised the whole of my attire. With a week's growth of beard, tousled hair and grimy hands and face, I could hardly recognise myself. . . ."

Our journalist-tramp checked in at St George's Crypt, a bleak but celebrated haven hard by Leeds Town Hall, but was soon transferred to a Church Army doss-house:

"The Town Hall clock chimed eleven, and shortly after the lights were extinguished. The busy hum of the streets subsided—and the dosshouse came to life. For almost an hour the sound of body-racking coughing, of hawking and spitting continued. One man about ten yards away was vomiting. A gentle sizzling snore went up to the roof and was followed by others of varying degrees of sound. Twelve o'clock came, and one o'clock, and the snores grew louder. I guessed it to be about four o'clock when I awakened feeling terribly cold, but I went to sleep again, and from about 6.30 the 'dosser' began to awaken. A new day was heralded by the scratch of matches and the flicker of lights as cigarettes began to be lit. 'What time is it Joe?' I heard a whisper. 'Quarter past seven—come on!' was the reply. The immediate creak of a bed signified that Joe's request was being met by action.

"At seven thirty, I pulled on my shoes, clothed myself fully and shuffled quietly along the corridor to the wash-basins. I washed myself, using my cap to dry my face, the calico towels being uninviting. I strayed through the door-way of the dining-room, where a lone eater greeted me. 'Are you from the Crypt?' he asked. 'Aye,' I answered. 'Fust night?' 'Aye'. 'Bundles of ruddy lousiness, that's what they are at that place. Never take their cloes off from one year end to another. People give 'em suits of cloes, thinking they're 'elping them wot's out of work, and it's them lousy b—— wot gets 'em.' He dug vindictively at a piece of bacon. . . ."

In the published version, intrepid "Grayson" took the train back sadder and wiser to Bradford. The family story is that he went first to Aunt Annie Bean's for a bath. "Cheeky thing," she said when he explained his mission, "coming here to leave your fleas!"

The *Pioneer* for which Feather wrote was the house journal of the Labour movement in Bradford (one of a string of local Labour weeklies of which the *Leeds Citizen* alone survived into the seventies). No one, from the editor downwards, was paid for his services. It was bought, read and sold by party and trade union activists. It projected the enthusiasms of its readers, or rather of those of its readers who were prepared to write for it. Before the First World War, J. B. Priestley contributed his first regular writing to the *Pioneer* ("As I knew noth-ing, I wrote about everything"). In the twenties and thirties, Jowett and Leach wrote weekly political columns; Betts expanded on literature, cricket and chess; a Bradford nurseryman provided both an advertisement and a gardening feature. The *Pioneer* used the national and provincial press as a source of news and comment—and belaboured the same papers as the voice of capitalism. Under Nichol's editorship, a *Pioneer* campaign provoked criminal charges against the leader of the Tory group on the city council, who was sent to prison for six months for steadily dipping his hand into the till at the Central Baths tea room. It nearly cost the editor his job as a school master. Feather himself was once threatened with a libel action by the *Yorkshire Observer* after he had exposed its readers' insurance scheme.

Feather branched out, too, into the *Daily Herald*, which was owned jointly by the TUC and Odhams Press. He wrote the main leader-page feature, adorned with an engraving of Orator Hunt, on 30 August 1933. The piece was headed: "Young Men—YOU are the Reformers of today." For his first appearance on a metropolitan stage, this was Vic the propagandist: "The rise of the Labour Party has meant that life today is a little less based on the law of the jungle than it was formerly. Even so, we realise that all this is not enough." And later: "A million of Socialist Youth, keen and eager, active and virile, throwing their weight and power on the side of the workers here would sound the death-knell of capitalism. . . . Within the League of Youth we can be a tower of strength for Socialism: and Socialism is the only hope for the world." Over to the left of the page, the editor was inveighing against "wage cut madness". Down below, Hannen Swaffer had been to see the first "stereoscopic movie". He wasn't sure it would last.

If Frank Betts cultivated Feather the writer and budding art-lover, Revis Barber, secretary of the Bradford Trades Council, nourished Feather the organiser. Alice

Barber, Revis's widow, remembers Feather dropping in "on his way home" at eleven o'clock and staying till one or two in the morning, when she would have to throw him out. There was, she says, a lot of leg-pulling, a lot of backchat, but Feather was also learning from Revis, who was fourteen years his senior.

They first worked together during the General Strike in 1926. Barber was then the assistant secretary of the trades council (his father was the secretary). The eighteen-year-old Feather was given the task of issuing the trades council's authority for the movement of food and emergency supplies. The council made the decisions, but Feather's signature was needed on the slip drivers had to produce if they were challenged by pickets.

Later, and with less of a nose for protocol, Feather contributed again to feeding the hungry. In the early thirties, with 20,000–30,000 registered unemployed in Bradford, Feather and a band of brothers—perhaps ten in all—would drive on to Ilkley Moors in an old, reconditioned lorry.

"There was one lad who'd been a butcher. That wasn't difficult, anyway, to get a butcher on a Wednesday afternoon when the shops were shut. We'd close in on a sheep and then we'd tackle it. And before you knew what had happened, the sheep was stuck, it was skinned. We took a spade with us so we could bury the fleece and the trotters. Then the carcass was on the lorry and we were back in Bradford. There was mutton broth and boiled mutton for two or three days after that."

The Robin Hoodlums of South Yorkshire had been up to similar butchery. Horace Green's father lived there, and Feather had been down to give them a hand. His story smacks now of a mating of Che Guevara and P. G. Wodehouse:

"The unemployed miners had been having mutton and mutton and mutton. Then they'd been having vegetable soup. I remember a discussion taking place. Somebody said, 'If only we could get some pork, that would make a change.' And they got round to talking about boiled ham. At that time we thought boiled ham was a real luxury. The only time you saw boiled ham was at funerals. Then somebody got the idea that there were a lot of pigs kept by the Earl of Fitzwilliam. And so the Bradford lads decided we'd help the miners to have some pork. We transferred our operations from Ilkley Moor to Wentworth Hall.

"We loaded up again, about ten of us. We worked out where the piggeries were, and we sent two lads over at the top of the piggeries, having marked out where we were going to knock the pig off. The two lads made one hell of a noise, and we heard the clatter of the herdsman's boots going past. Then we got busy on the pig, and this pig never had time to squeal it was so fast. And we were over the wall and on to the van.

"The poor herdsman—we never hurt him or anything like that, but he was overcome. He thought discretion was the better part of valour, and so he walked off. At that time communications weren't so brilliant, and the police weren't as mobile. When we got back, we thought there was something strange about this pig. There weren't many lights along the lanes as we went along, but he looked a very gloomy sort of pig. It turned out it was a black Berkshire pig. We were a bit astonished when about a week later there were notices all over the villages offering £25 reward for information about who'd killed this pig.

Apparently this pig was worth £250. This frightened us to death, because we thought that somebody would be bound to split, because of the reward, but nobody did split. Afterwards there was a lot of joking. Somebody said, 'If that was £250, it wasn't worth it.' Certainly, it was never meant for eating."

Feather was busy, too, in the Bradford Unemployed Workers' Committee, which was run by Revis Barber as a subcommittee of the trades council. These committees were established in 1932 at the request of the TUC, which was anxious to see "the welding of the forces of workers and would-be workers". Twenty years before Mrs Rosa Parks refused to give up her seat to a white passenger on a bus in Montgomery, Alabama, Feather can claim to have invented the sit-in as an instrument of political protest. The Bradford Unemployed Workers' Committee had raised a collection from open-air meetings in Bank Street. Feather gathered about 120 unemployed men, gave them fourpence each, and sent them into Brown Muffs, the city's most fashionable department store. The men were instructed to file into the café, the favourite meeting place of millowners' wives, sit down and order a cup of tea each.

The fourpences would just meet the bill. Then they were to stay put through tea time. The management accepted the unemployed, who bought their tea, filled the place, and stayed for an hour.

Until 1931, the focus of Feather's activity in the Labour movement was on the political rather than the industrial wing. The switch of interest came with the defection of MacDonald, Philip Snowden and J. H. Thomas in August 1931, and the formation of the

National Government. As Feather read events, only the solid sense of the unions prevented still more Labour MPs following the leadership into the wrong camp.

For Feather in Bradford, it was a matter of emphasis, rather than a break with politics. It was accelerated during the next year by the divorce of the Labour Party and the ILP. The conflict between the two was partly ideological: the ILP was less willing to compromise what it regarded as the essence of Socialism or the working-class interest (always a prickly issue when there is a Labour Government). More immediately, the division was over Parliamentary discipline. ILP members resisted the rule of standing orders. They insisted on the right to vote according to their consciences and in the interests of their constituents. The ILP returned to Bradford, the city of its birth, for the conference of July 1932, which voted to disaffiliate from the Labour Party.

Bradford had always been a stronghold of the ILP. All of its Labour councillors were ILP men. The ILP controlled a printing works, a cinema and the Jowett Hall. After the break between Labour and the ILP, most of the leading political figures went into the Labour Party. Jowett, by now an old and stubborn gladiator, was one of the handful who stood by the ILP. Feather went with the majority. He had opposed the break, which he interpreted as an attempt to establish a rival party of the Left. So long as the ILP remained an evangelical movement, he could see a useful role for it within the Labour Party. Once it broke away, it simply dissipated energies that could be put to better purpose elsewhere.

The split brought a souring of personal relations for Feather, and something more bitter for his elders in the movement. Hostility between the Labour Party and the rump ILP reached its height in the 1935 general election, when Wilf Heywood fought Jowett for his old seat of Bradford East. The Conservative won on a split vote.

Feather began now to give more of his time to his union, the National Union of Distributive and Allied Workers (later the Union of Shop, Distributive and Allied Workers). He was already a shop collector and had represented NUDAW on the trades council. After 1931 he was elected to the branch committee, and eventually became its chairman and representative on the Yorkshire divisional council. Power lay with the unions, though that didn't discourage Feather flirting with Parliament. He was interviewed by the Labour Party at Chester and was shortlisted at Shipley. He was handicapped by lack of union sponsorship. At one meeting he was asked how much he'd got. "If you mean money," the prospective candidate replied, "nothing. If you're talking about ability, more than any other candidate you've got on the shortlist." He did not get the nomination. Nor was he successful with applications for a job in his union. Membership was dropping, the staff was contracting, and organisers' posts were given first to men already working in union offices.

On 26 December 1930, Feather was married in Orford Parish Church, Warrington. He had met his bride five years earlier at a Co-operative Union summer school at Briarfields, near Burnley. Victor had won the scholarship from Bradford, Alice had won the scholarship from Warrington. For the most part it was courtship by correspondence, though now and again Feather would cycle from Bradford to Warrington to see her: a good fifty miles with the Pennines in between. They were married on Boxing Day, returning almost immediately to Bradford so that Victor could be back at work within forty-eight hours. It is a marriage that has endured, producing a son (now an official of the Iron and Steel Trades Confederation), a daughter and a small tribe of grandchildren. Feather's public and private lives have, however, touched only at tangents—and there has been precious little private life.

CHAPTER FIVE

London and a white collar

THE LABOUR MOVEMENT has its own talent web as surely as the City of London or the Brigade of Guards. Quite independently, both of the men who appointed Victor Feather to the TUC in 1937 knew about him in advance and hoped he would be persuaded to apply. Walter Citrine, the general secretary, tried to find Feather before the job was advertised in the *Daily Herald*. His assistant, Vincent Tewson, sat tight and waited for Feather's application to come in. It was not a question of nepotism or influence, but of senior men in a still small and flexible office noting someone with the qualities likely to be useful to them.

Citrine had spotted Feather at a weekend school in Yorkshire. The TUC general secretary reviewed the movement's problems and future. His lecture was followed by an animated discussion. Feather's recollection of his own contribution is that he was very critical, even rude. None the less, Citrine was impressed by the young man with fair hair, fresh complexion and tweed sports jacket. He thought him incisive and down-to-earth. He kept him in mind, and a few months later decided that this was the kind of man he wanted to expand the TUC's organisation department.

The difficulty was that he did not have Feather's name. So Citrine wrote to one of the organisers of the weekend school, described the young man, and asked for his name and address. His letter gave no indication of the business he was about. The general secretary was given a name and fixed an appointment. The man was sent his fare and a subsistence allowance, but still was given no hint of why he was being invited 200 miles from Bradford to see Citrine. The interview was fixed for an afternoon. Citrine's secretary announced the young man's name, and he walked in. It was the wrong man, but not only the wrong man. It was a blind man, and, mistaken identity apart, a blind man could not have done the sort of work the TUC wanted: reading and typing papers, travelling about the country, tangling with employers and union rebels. On the spur of the moment, Citrine had to conjure some reason for having brought this man to London. He asked him about the value of weekend schools. From his experience, how could they be improved as a service to union members? After an improvised half-hour, Citrine thanked him profusely and packed him back to Bradford.

Tewson had no such problems of identification. He had known Feather's father in Bradford. Although he had gone to London twelve years earlier, he went home occasionally and looked in at the East Ward Labour Club. Old friends there had talked about Victor Feather as a rising public speaker and organiser. When the TUC was looking for an assistant in the organisation department, Tewson remembered Feather, "a practical sort of chap, with his roots right". The assistant general secretary was tempted to drop him a note about the job, but thought better of it. Feather must not feel he had a friend at court.

Although Citrine tried afresh to find the young man of the weekend school, he evidently failed. The organisation department post was advertised, and Feather was among the dozens of applicants. He made the short list and was invited to Transport House, which the TUC then shared with the Labour Party and the Transport and General Workers. But the catalogue of coincidences was not finished. One of his fellow-passengers on the train to London was Revis Barber, who was also on the short list. According to Feather, they bumped into each other on the platform at King's Cross and realised for the first time that they were rivals for the same job. With years of trades council organisation behind him, Barber was full of hope. Bradford veterans say he was deeply disappointed when he was passed over and young Feather landed the job, though it seems to have left no scar on their personal relationship. Thirteen years later, Feather went back to Bradford as assistant secretary of the TUC to present Barber with the Silver Badge of Congress for his twenty-one years as secretary of the trades council.

Feather was appointed in April 1937. He finished work at Greengates Co-op on the Saturday night, travelled to London on the Sunday, and began his duties at the TUC on the Monday morning. Everything was different. Even the climate: Feather went south in an overcoat. He did not need it again till November. Housing a family was different. By now the Feathers had a toddling daughter, Pat, who stayed in Bradford with her mother till father found them somewhere to live. In Bradford they had a council house; in London there was none available. Feather had about £50 of savings, which he hoped would be enough for a deposit. He saw some flats advertised in Marsham Street, round the corner from his Westminster office. The price was £425, which he thought he might just afford—till he discovered that was a year's rent, about £3 a week more than his salary of £5. Then he learned

ANTHONIUS GADIUS: I have prepared them for the sacrifice

UNREHEARSED INCIDENT

THE ORATOR: " Just thinking won't alter your rotten conditions. You've got to join a Trade Union and ACT! "

Two cartoons by Vic Feather

Two drawings by Vic Feather: an early advertisement on the left, and *Punch* cover dated 3 May 1972 on right

the lesson of all provincials in London: add the rent to the fares, then work out how near the centre you can afford to live. Feather did his sums, checked the Underground timetables, and rode out to Hounslow West. It was the end of a line with a last train at 12.32, very handy for a man who expected to work irregular hours. He put down 5 per cent on a house costing £695. It was new and semi-detached. Alice and Pat came down in the van with the furniture, and the Feathers have lived there ever since.

But the biggest difference was the work. At twenty-nine Feather had always worked on his feet. At the TUC he was to spend much of his day in a chair. On his first day, he went out for a man-sized lunch, came back to his papers, and almost fell asleep at his desk. Tewson suggested that he spend a week or ten days reading himself in. "When he came back," Tewson says, "it was obvious that he was living in another world. But he was intensely interested in what he had been reading. He used to slam away learning to type. He confessed to me many years afterwards that he had never worked so hard in his life as when he was preparing to do that job."

Feather's immediate chief was Edgar Harries, who had previously run the organisation department single-handed. Harries was a Pembrokeshire man, a former shipwright and the son of a Congregational minister. He had been the founder secretary of the Labour Party in the county, and joined the TUC research department in 1928. Feather found him a tough administrator and a martinet. He gave orders and resented "impertinence". Feather feared he was going to get the sack in his first week. Harries complained that he didn't like having to share an office. Feather replied that he would rather be on his own too. Harries was not amused.

E

Feather's assignment was trades councils and the organisation of manual workers. A second assistant, appointed to Harries' staff soon after Feather, handled local government and white-collar work. The lines were not drawn too sharply. Feather advised trades councils on anything and everything: how to approach the town hall; what their legal status was. But he came at the same time to be regarded as a jack of all trades. He was given most of the jobs that didn't fit into anyone else's department. Where there was trouble, Feather was sent—either to clear it up, or to prepare the ground for someone with more authority. "Victor," as Tewson testifies, "would always have a bash at anything." Feather's first big job was the fight for union recognition at the Ford Motor Company. Fords would not recognise the unions, and men joining a union tended to be edged out. Feather's task was to coordinate the efforts of the different unions. He would go down to Dagenham or one of the other Essex works by train in the morning and frequently arrive home in Hounslow after midnight.

The trades council brief gave Feather his first professional brush with the Communists. The Fascist and Communist parties had been proscribed by the TUC. Congress and the general council had deemed their members unfit to be delegates to trades councils or to hold office in those councils. The Communists were the most obvious "threat". They were making capital out of the United Front activities and the Spanish Civil War. The trades councils were a prime and vulnerable target. Feather's rôle was to strengthen the resistance of trades councils that were under pressure from Communist-dominated union branches, or to coax heretical councils back into congress line.

As a junior official, Feather had few levers to use against the Communists. He would attend trades council meetings and stand the TUC's ground. The meetings were often stormy. Since the Communists could not vent their spleen against Citrine or the general council, they took it out on Feather. And Feather, with the soapbox years behind him, answered in kind. He made his biggest mistake one night at Watford in 1938. He had been told to throw someone out of a trades council, and took the order literally, hoisting two recalcitrants through the swing doors. The Communists and the local press had a field day. Lurid cuttings were sent by the party to every member of the general council—by registered post to home and office addresses. Feather was summoned to explain himself to Citrine, and was lucky to escape with a warning. With a modicum more tact, he continued the fight into 1940. It proved, however, to be a mere preliminary skirmish for the sustained campaign Feather waged at a more senior level in the late forties and fifties.

Although Feather's TUC work was absorbing, it did not exclude all other activity. He went for a while to Harold Laski's informal economics classes, and he helped to organise support for the Republican side in the Spanish Civil War. Feather had known men in the West Riding who went to fight, but he was reminded of his family responsibilities when he thought of joining them. His sympathies were for the POUM (Partido Obrero de Unificación Marxista), led by Joaquín Maurín and defined by Hugh Thomas in his Civil War history as "Marxist opponents of Stalin who shared Trotsky's general views: permanent revolution abroad, working-class collectivism at home". After he moved south, Feather was threatened with police prosecution for defacing the pavement by chalking political cartoons—Franco, Baldwin, *et al.*—in Hounslow High Street and for holding an unauthorised street collection, for the Spanish Socialists. The case was never pursued.

Feather was in a reserved occupation and was not called up for service in the Second World War, but he joined the Home Guard. During the London blitz, he saved three people from a bombed shelter and was awarded a certificate for bravery. It was presented on 1 January 1942, to Volunteer Victor G. H. Feather, "A" Company, 2nd Middlesex Battalion, Home Guard. The citation read:

"On the night of 19th October, 1940, Vol. Feather was instrumental in saving the lives of three of the four occupants of a wrecked concrete shelter. During a heavy air raid on that night the shelter was demolished by the blast and fragmentation from the explosion of a nearby bomb and, in addition, it was completely covered with debris from adjoining shattered houses.

"Under very difficult conditions, and at great personal risk, Vol. Feather laboured unceasingly for some hours, during the raid and afterwards, and despite the seeming hopelessness of his task, he ultimately succeeded in safely extricating all four buried persons, three only of whom were still alive. Vol. Feather's bravery and devotion to the work of rescue were outstanding."

The war brought the TUC into partnership with the Coalition Government. First priority was to defeat the Germans, and Ernest Bevin at the Ministry of Labour was determined to exploit the skills and influence of the trade union movement. Feather's part was still a junior one. He was promoted "Secretary of the Trades Councils Department", but it remained a sub-department and he remained subordinate to Harries. Citrine used Feather to do the devilling for Bevin's Joint Consultative Committee, the meeting-point of Government, employers and unions, and as a troubleshooter. He was regarded as a man who could use his own initiative, without constantly returning for further instructions. If a strike was hindering the war effort, Feather would be dispatched to smooth it out. Girls at a factory in Ipswich who would not work with another group of girls; men on building sites or airfields; unions disputing demarcation lines. It was another apprenticeship, this time in the subtleties of conciliation, the brimstone and honey that were to be his trademark in more elevated days.

At the end of 1941, a Soviet trade union delegation came to Britain as guests of the TUC and with the blessing of Churchill and his Foreign Secretary, Anthony Eden. The Government was keen to foster Anglo-Soviet co-operation, and Citrine had dreams of a link between the trade union movements of Britain, America and Russia. Moscow sent nine delegates, an interpreter, and three burly male "secretaries". They stayed for six weeks, visiting ten cities and about sixty factories, shipyards and coal mines. The Russians were divided into three groups, each with its own TUC shepherd. Ernest Bell, of the international department, had one group; Albert Carthy, later general secretary of the Socialist International, had another; and Feather a third.

Citrine found his visitors "very human, once they had become throughly acquainted with us". Feather had no trouble separating the aims of our Soviet allies from the aims of his old sparring partners the Communist Party of Great Britain; learned a smattering of Russian on his travels; and was bowled over by one of the delegates, Klavdia Nikolayeva. "She was," he says, "a very powerful woman, one of the most dynamic women I have ever met. I wouldn't say she was beautiful, but she was an extraordinary woman and a kind woman, although she could be tough."

The Russians were given a full clothing ration and eagerly bought clothes, blankets, razors and anything else they could carry for themselves and their friends and families back home. Their TUC hosts tried to ensure that they were not cheated.

"Victor Feather reported to me a nasty incident," Citrine records in his autobiography. "One of the delegation showed him a watch for which he had paid £10, and which, in Feather's opinion, was not worth more than from £3 to £5 at the outside. Another had a watch worth still less, for which he had paid £11 10s. It looked as though they had been rooked. Feather, with his usual energy and initiative, got in touch with the London Chamber of Commerce, who, in turn, enabled him to contact the sole agent for the manufacturers of these watches, which happened to have been imported. After examining them, he declared that one watch was not worth more than £5, allowing for purchase tax and a fair profit to the retailer, and the other was definitely second-hand and worth about thirty shillings. This was the one for which £11 10s had been paid and for which the retailer had given a spurious guarantee. Both had been bought from the same shop but at different times. The agent took Feather along and together they interviewed the retailer, who shamefacedly but speedily repaid the full amount he had received for the two watches."

Feather himself offers a less punctilious version of this denouement: "The agent recognised the tradesman immediately and said, 'Oh dear, Charlie, it's you again is it? Different name, different name.' And he said, 'Come on, you sold this, chuck it. Just hand over the money.' And the fellow just handed it over."

One night Feather and Albert Carthy were staying with the Russians in the Hyde Park Hotel. One of the groups had come back from the Midlands with a couple of bicycles that had been presented to them at the Hercules factory. The two shepherds were woken after midnight by an anguished hotel manager. The Russians were taking it in turns to try their skill along the upstairs corridor, and most of them weren't very proficient. "They kept falling off and hitting doors," Feather recalls. "It just seemed like a drunken man staggering along the corridor. Distressed ladies and very choleric gentlemen were opening doors and saying, 'Good gracious, whatever is happening? We'll tell the manager!'"

The Russians' final stop was in Glasgow, where they were to embark on a warship home. Their presence was supposed to be top secret, but after days of cinemagoing (Deanna Durbin and Bing Crosby) and a visit to Clydebank, the word must have been spreading. The delegation left in a British cruiser, but it was accidentally rammed by a troopship in the darkness and put back into port. Citrine was alerted "in the strictest wartime secrecy" by the Admiralty, and immediately sent Feather to Glasgow. His mission was to make the Russians comfortable and to "ensure the fullest secrecy about the delegation's presence, more particularly so now in view of the collision". With the permission of their leader, S. M. Shvernik, Feather took them on another shopping expedition. "After about an hour's steady shopping," Citrine writes, "two sharp-eyed Glasgow urchins said to Feather, 'Mister, aren't these the two women from Russia?' The shopping expedition was brought to a quick conclusion." The delegation sailed on the cruiser *Cario* on 9 February 1942. "According to Feather," Citrine again records, "everybody was just a little subdued at the leavetaking, and Madame Nikolayeva, one of the oldest and toughest members of the party, embraced him vigorously in front of a group of grinning sailors."

Sixteen months later, Feather went to the Soviet Union with the TUC's return delegation—Citrine and two members of the general council, Harry Harrison and Andrew Conley. They flew a tortuous route, across the Mediterranean and the Near East, by RAF Liberator bomber. It was Feather's second trip abroad. He had spent a week's holiday in Germany a couple of years before joining the TUC, seeing Nazism at first hand and bearing clandestine greetings from old comrades in the ILP.

On the last leg of the TUC party's flight from Teheran to Moscow, their Liberator came under fire over the Caspian Sea. Feather remembers seeing a puff or two of smoke and thinking they were small clouds. "All of a sudden I saw a puff of smoke, and then it had a red centre, and suddenly the aircraft started being showered with what seemed like heavy hailstones. I realised we were being met with anti-aircraft fire. There were about ten or fifteen shells put up at us, and they were much too near for comfort. It was one of the most fascinating things I've ever seen—to see a burst of smoke and realise that was a shell exploding with a beautiful red heart less than 200 yards away."

The flight engineer—"a bit superstitious; he always wore one of his wife's stockings around his throat on a flight"—rushed aft, exclaiming cheerfully: "This is just like the old days when we were going over Germany." He told Citrine that they were passing over a convoy of tankers with a destroyer at their head. The pilot had been challenged by the destroyer to give the day's signal and had replied with a red Very light. "It was not the destroyer which had fired at us," Citrine writes, "but the tankers, who had not waited for an assurance that we were a friendly aircraft."

Like the Russians in Britain, the TUC team saw factories and factories and more factories, travelling from Moscow into the Urals and Siberia. Feather noted that the works in the Urals were manned by people who "looked as if they had just fallen off camels in Uzbekistan", a peasant population trying to do skilled work and not entirely succeeding. In the Don basin, the visitors were taken to a primitive coal mine and invited to descend to the face. It meant climbing down a narrow hole by a wooden ladder for thirty feet, then crawling on their stomachs. The two general councillors preferred to wait at the top. Citrine and the ever-loyal Feather went below.

To balance Crosby and Durbin, Citrine's party was taken to watch Dynamo play Zenith and to see *Swan Lake* at the Bolshoi. Before the football match, the general secretary was introduced to both teams in the Dynamo Stadium. The two captains presented him with a bouquet, which Citrine accepted with public grace and private unease. Bouquets were for women. As soon as he could, he passed the flowers on to Feather, the secretary to the delegation, who clung to them for the rest of the day under the stiletto eye of their Russian guide. At the Bolshoi that night the audience went into raptures at the end of the first act. Feather looked swiftly at the guide, then threw the bouquet at the prima ballerina's feet. The guide nodded approvingly, then pointed to the Dynamo card still tied to the stems. Feather had forgotten to take it off.

CHAPTER SIX

The sport of Greeks

ON 12 JANUARY 1945, Citrine called on Winston
Churchill at No. 10 Downing Street. It was a routine
working visit, but instead of discussing appointments to
Government committees as Citrine had expected, the
Prime Minister launched immediately into a review of the
situation in Greece. The last of the occupying Germans
had been driven out the previous October, but the liberation was soon followed by civil war. Towards the end of
December, Churchill and Eden visited Athens and
restored a precarious order, backed by British troops.
Within days the British Ambassador, Reginald Leeper,
received a deputation of Greek trade unionists who asked
for a TUC delegation to visit Greece. Churchill strongly
urged Citrine to co-operate, and after a brief show of
war-weary reluctance, the general secretary agreed to
lead a delegation. So was born Victor Feather's first major
assignment for the international trade union movement,
five months entangled in the dangerous Greek national
sport of politics. By the end of June he had been (literally)
under fire; signed two laws into the Statute Book; and
carved a fragile pattern out of the chaos of Greek trade
unionism.

"Politically the workers were profoundly divided
among themselves," the International Labour Organisation recorded in a clinical review of Greek trade unionism

published twenty-one years later. "The main obstacle to a
rapid reconstruction of the trade union movement was the
extreme division existing in the movement itself, as
expressed in rival tendencies which had been exacerbated
by the insurrection. At the time of the liberation there
were a large number of trends, both Right-Wing and
Left-Wing. The actual scale of these could not be
determined in the absence of elections, but all had their
origin as much in personal ambition as in ideological
differences. A desperate struggle to control the trade
union movement was the natural consequence. . . . The
problem, therefore, was to find a place in the provisional
executive committee for representatives of all tendencies,
to induce them to co-operate honestly in organising elections, and finally to make them accept the results of
elections with a good grace."

Citrine's TUC delegation returned from Athens at the
beginning of February 1945, with a more shell-shocked
appraisal. "We found, almost right up to the end of our
visit, bitterness and hostility between those who had sided
with the Greek Government, and those who had attached
themselves to the bodies opposing the Government.
Charges of collaboration with the Metaxas dictatorship,
and charges of collaboration with the Germans, were so
numerous that it was utterly impossible for us to embark
upon the necessary factual and careful examination, which
would have enabled us to have pronounced a definite
opinion upon them.

"That does not mean that we did not examine any
charges. We were compelled to by force of circumstances.
We had to listen to a great deal of recrimination which
did not in the least contribute to a settlement of the differences. We heard charges of terrorism levelled against the

former Greek Confederation of Labour, whose representatives were Kalomiris, Stratis, Theos and Mariolis, who, throughout recent events, had given their support to EAM (Greek National Front of Liberation) in its policy of opposition to the present Greek Government. No charges of terrorism were levelled against the group recognised by the present Minister of Labour, and which is headed by Hadjidimitriou, but counter-charges of collaboration with the Metaxas dictatorship and the German occupying authorities were made."

Citrine's party spent a fortnight in Greece. For all the belligerence, it did achieve a first, tentative agreement between the rival factions. A second TUC team was sent in its wake. It was led by Vincent Tewson, the assistant general secretary, who was accompanied by Bert Papworth, a Communist TGWU member of the general council, and Feather. Tewson persuaded the Greek trade unionists to sign a second agreement on 25 Feburary, which added clauses on elections and the reorganisation of the provisional executive of the Confederation of Labour. Feather was then left to translate pieces of paper into electoral reality. His task had been made intractable by the history of the preceding decade. Under the Metaxas dictatorship, from 1936 to 1941, trade unions were centralised and controlled by the Government. Freedom of association was eclipsed. The German occupation, from 1941 to 1944, merely completed the process. All trade union activity was paralysed.

Feather arrived in Athens on a cold February day with a Utility suit, the rank of colonel, and a room in the Grande Bretagne, the capital's ritziest hotel, which was then the British military headquarters. He found at least five trade union factions, ranging from "Monarcho-Fascists" on the

Right to Communists on the Left. The Monarcho-Fascists resisted the designation, though their history suggested they came very close to deserving it. Things were made no easier by the different groups' knack of striking temporary and shifting alliances, like pieces in a kaleidoscope held by a man in an advanced state of *delirium tremens*.

If his efforts were to carry any conviction, Feather had to assess town by town, sometimes factory by factory, the real strength of the rival factions. He had two interpreters, one a Greek civil servant, the other a British soldier of Greek origin called Generapolos. But he soon acquired a working knowledge of demotic Greek. At the British Embassy one evening, the Ambassador overheard him trying the language and rounded on the young men of his staff. "You've all been to university, you've all been taught Greek, and there's Feather here who's been here only two months and he speaks better Greek than any of you," he said. "Yes," one of the Greek women guests intervened, "but what Greek!"

The trade union factions all claimed thousands and thousands of members. Under the dictatorship and the occupation, "membership" had been compulsory. Subscriptions were deducted at source for the Government-controlled unions. This meant that any figures based on this "membership" were artificial and inflated. All claims had to be proved, and in the prevailing climate no one could be trusted to probe on Feather's behalf. He had to travel the length and breadth of Greece, attending meetings organised by "trades councils", and probe for himself.

Verification inevitably was rough and ready, but Feather was armed with the shrewdness of a lifetime in the Labour movement and eight years' troubleshooting for the

TUC. If one faction claimed predominance in a particular district, he would ask where its membership was concentrated. "Right," he would say, "let's go and see." Then he would take the supposed leaders to the factory and see the reception they attracted from the workers. The Hadjidimitriou faction, for example, claimed to represent all the tobacco workers. So Feather put them on a platform and gauged their welcome, which turned out to be pretty thin. Then he repeated the operation with the Theos faction, which was applauded to the Doric skies. That, though, was not the end of the assessment. Feather had to check that the meetings had not been packed. How many men worked in the factory? How many had turned up for the meeting? Ultimately it was a matter of instinct and judgment. Feather learned to go not just by what people said or shouted, but how they looked when they said or shouted it.

Some of the messages were clearer than others. Feather saw guns brandished three times during his Greek mission. On the first occasion Feather and Papworth were walking along a main street one night in Athens. The lights were blacked out and a curfew had been imposed, but as British "colonels" the TUC men had passes to go out. "We were coming round a corner," Feather remembers, "and a fellow just jumped out of a doorway with a pistol and jammed it in my ribs and started talking. I immediately started speaking English, and when he realised I was English the gunman backed off and I got out of the way quick."

Later Feather was being driven in an army jeep on the road from Athens to Megara. There were no buses, or trains, or private cars. As the jeep with the Union Jack and "TUC" painted on its flank passed, a man sprang on to the road and fired at it with a rifle. The shot missed, but Feather did not stop to ask him who he was or why he was shooting. He ordered the army driver to put his foot down and hoped there was no gunman around the next bend.

The third experience of gunplay came at a meeting of union factions Feather had summoned in an Athens hotel. "It was very long," he says, "and they were snarling at me across the table. They got very vicious. There was no sort of conversation or discussion, there was denunciation. One fellow leapt to his feet and was denouncing the other side at the top of his voice, teeth flashing, eyes flashing. And I thought well, this is Greece so we'll just let it boil itself out. And all of a sudden he pulled a gun, and before any-one knew what was happening everybody was on their feet, and everybody in that room had a gun except me. One shot went—it wasn't shot at me, perhaps it was some sort of an indication, anyway it went into the wall. So I hammered on the table with a gavel. I thought that was the appropriate thing to do, and they were rather aston-ished. And I said, 'Please will you sit down', in Greek, and I think that this astonished them as well. And they put their pistols away. I made it quite clear through the interpreter that next time they came into a meeting they should leave their guns outside. What they did outside was up to them, but they shouldn't bring their pistols inside with them. They thought that this was rather a joke. Both parties dissolved into laughter at this idea, and we carried on with the meeting."

Eventually, by the end of April, the trade union factions agreed on the composition of a new provisional executive for their confederation. Of its twenty-one members, eleven belonged to the Reformist group, four to the Socialists, four to the Communists, and two to the Trade

Union (Revolutionary) group. Under what became known as the First Feather Agreement, the parties also agreed to ask the Minister of Labour, Sideris, to introduce by legislation a system of proportional representation in the trade union organisations. A second Feather Agreement in June provided for the executive to take all necessary measures to enable a union congress to meet by 10 September.

Legislation was less easy to obtain than to request. Greek Governments were so ephemeral in 1945 that no one would take responsibility for putting laws of a contentious nature on the Statute Book. Feather went to see the Regent, Archbishop Damaskinos, tall and black-bearded in the manner of the Orthodox priesthood. He suggested that if Feather wanted his laws he'd better sign them himself. The Regent was evidently worried that he might be exceeding his own powers. Feather said he had no constitutional authority, but the Archbishop persisted. If the Regent agreed and the trade unions agreed, why didn't he go ahead? Nobody would accuse Feather of wanting to usurp the power of Parliament. On the grounds that nothing that united everyone from Monarcho-Fascists to Communists could be bad, the junior official of the TUC solemnly signed.

Feather's last problem was to find a leader for the newly unified Greek Confederation of Labour. He hit on Fotis Makris, an earnest official young enough to be untainted by the years of dictatorship and occupation. His experience was limited, but Feather found him energetic and quick to learn, with the agile mind of a man who could live in Greek politics. Makris was elected general secretary of the confederation, an office he continued to hold until after the Colonels' coup of 1967.

Russian trade
union delegation
visiting tailoring
factory. Feather
centre back row

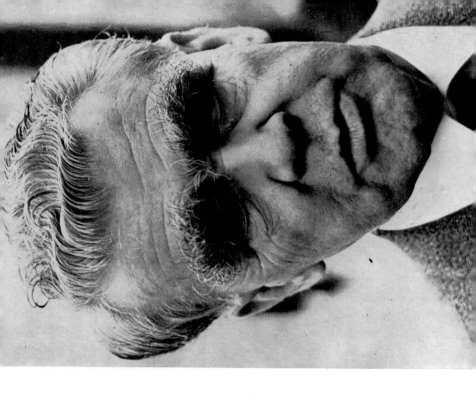

Sir Vincent Tewson 1958 (*left*)
George Woodcock as general secretary (*right*)

The success of Feather's mission was hailed by British newspapers as diverse as the *Daily Worker* and the *Daily Telegraph*. "Trade union unity has been achieved in Greece," the *Worker*'s correspondent reported on 11 May. A mass meeting of 35,000 workers had adopted a joint resolution urging an increased standard of living, complete freedom for the trade union movement, dissolution of all armed terrorist organisations, and an immediate purge of Fascist elements from the State machinery and punishment of collaborators. "Mr Victor Feather," the Communist daily added, "presided at the meeting and was wildly cheered when he announced that he brought the greetings of eight million British workers."

On the same day Richard Capell, of the *Daily Telegraph*, wrote of the "personal success of Mr Victor Feather, who has induced the Greek trade unionists to sink their differences". Capell was more cautious in another dispatch, filed on 29 June: "Mr Victor Feather left for Britain today. Temporarily at least, the aim laid down five months ago by Sir Walter Citrine, general secretary of the TUC, appears to have been achieved. Sir Walter then urged the Greek unions to work towards the establishment of the principle that social questions, not national politics, were the unions' proper concern. It remains to be seen whether the deep-seated resentments caused by the Communists' executions of 140 trade union leaders last December have been removed. Elections for the Greek TUC begin next month. It is noteworthy, that 83 per cent of the trade unionists abstained from voting at separate union elections in recent months. The explanation given is fear of intimidation by extremists."

F

The *Telegraph* correspondent's reservations were well-grounded. The Greek union congress did not take place by 10 September, as stipulated in the Second Feather Agreement. It required a further meeting on 2 December for the various tendencies to accept and respect the results of the union elections. The chairman at the meeting was Louis Saillant, general secretary of the World Federation of Trade Unions, which had been founded in London in February 1945, and at that stage brought together Communist and non-Communist unions. Feather was at Saillant's right hand.

In the words of the ILO's 1966 survey, "As a result of this series of preliminary agreements, freely entered into between the various trade union tendencies, all possible guarantees seemed to exist for ensuring the reconstruction of the Greek trade union movement on a really democratic basis." In fact, the Greek Confederation of Labour fell apart again within the year. Léon Jouhaux, the veteran French trade union leader, was sent to Athens in July 1946, with a brief from the WFTU to try yet again. Feather had laid the foundations. Only the Greeks could build the house.

CHAPTER SEVEN

Travels of a trade union organiser

VICTOR FEATHER played a more peripheral part in the postwar restoration of democratic trade unions in Western Germany. In Greece he had been for the most part on his own in an exclusively British operation. In Germany he was one of an international trade union team working under the occupying Powers. Feather's involvement began in a seemingly casual way in 1944, a full year before the end of the war in Europe. Edgar Harries, the head of the TUC organisation department, called him in and asked for some ideas for reorganising a trade union movement, or even for starting one from scratch. It could have been for the West Indies, perhaps, or India. Germany was not mentioned at that stage. Feather went away and prepared a blueprint. The pattern he proposed was one of industrial unionism—the ideal towards which Britain was still groping three decades later of one union representing all the workers in any industry. It was not a startlingly original notion, even in 1944, but Country X could be spared the craft rivalries and interests inseparable from the slow evolution of trade unionism in Britain.

Taking as his model the union he knew best—the shopworkers—Feather recommended that each industrial union should allow representation for different sections with different needs and points of view. Manual and clerical workers, in the simplest division, should have opportunities for discussing their development and contributing to union policy, just as the butchers, the bakers and the candlestick-makers had in NUDAW. Again taking a familiar model, Feather suggested that the trade union movement should comprise sixteen or seventeen of these huge industrial unions, following roughly the trade groups of the TUC. There would be one union for mining, one for engineering, one for textiles and so on.

Feather's draft was no more than an internal memorandum. He submitted it to Harries, who in turn submitted it with his own recommendations to Citrine. The document was not published, and in its original form probably was never discussed by the general council. But when Citrine went to Berlin in January 1946, as leader of a delegation from the World Federation of Trade Unions, he pressed the case for "a structure which would result in a single trades union in each industry, covering all the workers of that industry in each of the zones". Feather's proposals had become TUC policy and ultimately WFTU policy, and the pattern was adopted for the revived West German trade union movement. In this case, the initiative seems to have come less from the Government than from Citrine's anticipation of the rôle the TUC would be expected and qualified to play in the postwar reconstruction.

Five years after he had completed his test-piece for Edgar Harries, Feather was sent to Germany to help with the practical implications. The TUC—and Feather—had kept in touch with developments during the early years of the Allied occupation. Much of the spade work was being done by R. W. Luce, an official of the Ministry of Labour who had been seconded to the British administration as head of the Manpower Division. In the British zone, at least, Luce was more responsible than anyone for developing an industrial relations system that eliminated the Nazi inheritance.

By 1949 the paramount need was for a corps of officials to run the new, democratic trade unions. Most of the old guard had either died in the concentration camps, built new lives in exile, or compromised themselves by co-operating with the Nazis. A handful, like Ludwig Rosenberg and Otto Brenner, who had taken refuge in Britain, returned to Germany. Rosenberg became head of the DGB's international department and eventually the movement's president. In any case, it was nearly twenty years since Hitler had taken power. The trade unions inevitably were short of people under thirty-five with any experience of democratic practice. To meet this need, the Allied Control Commission established training courses in association with the German unions and the international trade union movement.

Feather was sent to Berlin by the TUC to work with the two German trade union federations, UGO and the DGB. He gave lectures and seminars to groups of about twenty young officials on the nuts and bolts of democratic trade unionism: the functions of unions, branches, shop stewards' committees, trades councils; the mechanics of consultation and ballots. Feather was there for about six weeks teaching at the Leuschnerhaus, the centre named after one of the heroes of German labour. Twenty years on, he was still meeting its graduates at international or German trade union conferences.

The TUC also sent Feather twice to France after the war. In 1945 Citrine wanted to check on the revival of trade unionism there. Feather went briefly to Paris, making contact with Léon Jouhaux and his Communist joint general secretary, Benoit Frachon. Citrine apart, Jouhaux was the first giant of the international trade union movement Feather had met. Jouhaux, who had spent the war in Nazi hands in Germany, was a burly figure with the pointed beard of a film Frenchman. Feather found him "weighty both in his thinking and his appearance".

Prophecy was none too difficult in liberation France. Feather recognised quickly enough that the Communists had been organising not just for resistance to the Germans, but for taking over as much as they could once the war was won. His instincts told him that Jouhaux would be propped in the shop window, while Frachon did the real work behind the scenes. Feather predicted that when the Communists calculated the time was ripe, they would pull down the blinds on the old leader. This proved correct. Jouhaux was pushed out. The Force Ouvrière, the Socialist trade union federation he then founded, has never competed in power and influence with the Communist CGT, of which Frachon became the first general secretary.

A year later, Feather returned to Paris as bag-carrier to the TUC representative invited by Ernest Bevin as part of the British delegation to the peace conference. Citrine had been snubbed in 1945 when, during a visit to the United States, he had asked to be attached to the British team at the first session of the United Nations in San Francisco, and was refused. The TUC general secretary blamed Clement Attlee and Ernest Bevin as much as their Conservative partners. But in July 1946, Bevin—now Foreign Secretary in a Labour Government—honoured the TUC with a seat at the conference table when twenty-one Allied nations met in the Palais de Luxembourg to draft peace treaties with Italy, Rumania, Hungary,

Bulgaria and Finland. The general council sent its chairman, Charlie Dukes, of the General and Municipal Workers, with Feather as his batman. The young official was shaken—and more than a little delighted—at the luxury that was paraded for the peace delegates. An opening of eyes and taste-buds after the years of rationing and austerity.

The TUC has always been pragmatic about its relations with governments or international institutions. Of Feather's next three overseas sorties, one was arranged with the Foreign Office, another with the Commonwealth Relations Office, and the third with the International Transport Workers' Federation and the International Confederation of Free Trade Unions. It is argued that so long as the aims are agreed, there is no reason why the unions should not collaborate. The aims, in Feather's postwar missions and in those of the fifties, were principally to foster trade unionism and to encourage the growth of democracy. Provided the Government did not try to dictate the form of trade unionism or the sort of contact the TUC should make, there were no inhibitions. The TUC generally makes a point of paying its own way.

In January and February, 1957, Feather toured South-East Asia. He lectured about trade unionism; visited national centres in India, Pakistan, Ceylon, Burma, Thailand and Singapore; met union officers; called on Ministers of Labour. He was showing the flag—for Britain and for trade unionism.

Later that year, Feather spent ten days in Japan settling a national railway strike. The stripling Japanese trade union movement had sounded an SOS, and Feather was dispatched to the rescue with Bob Coutts, an officer of one of the American railroad unions. Coutts had no international experience, but Feather found him a shrewd man—and happily a man who liked paper work. So Coutts took the notes and wrote the report while Feather got on with the negotiating.

The first thing they discovered when they reached Tokyo was that the entire leadership of the Japanese railway union had been thrown into jail. Evidently the strike was against the law, though imprisoning the national officers and executive was not helping the stock to roll. After a quick briefing from the Labour Attaché at the British Embassy, Feather sought an interview with the Prime Minister.

"Mr Kishi was the Prime Minister, Mr Ishi was the Deputy Prime Minister, and Mr Ishida was the Minister of Labour. So I didn't have to rack my brains very much for names—Kishi, Ishi, Ishida—and this was what I said virtually all the day, and I got to see these people. I saw Kishi and he said that he was in favour of what I was proposing and would I see Mr Ishi. And I saw Mr Ishi and he referred me to Mr Ishida. And when I got to Mr Ishida he wouldn't move without Mr Ishi, and Mr Ishi wouldn't move without Mr Kishi, and I was chasing up and down for three days."

But Feather did get the union leaders out of jail—on the undertaking that once they were free and negotiations were under way, the strikers would go back to work. The rescue party had no authority for this promise, but the union leaders stood by it when they were released. The railways started running, and after a few more sixteen-hour days Feather and Coutts induced a settlement, packed their bags and fled the land. If the settlement came unstuck, someone else would have to repair it. Fortunately it did not come unstuck.

Feather returned to Asia in 1959 when he spent six weeks in India trying to improve working relations between the Socialist and Communist trade union organisations. As in Greece, he travelled the country testing attitudes and contacts and attempting to create an atmosphere in which the rival leaders could come together. His visit worked no magic. No one had expected that it would. The two organisations remain apart. The most that can be claimed is that after his stay, the two sides found they could talk to each other.

Although Feather likes to pose as the bluff Englishman, even as the stage Yorkshireman, a sort of working-class Freddie Trueman, he is not an insular man. He enjoys the company of foreigners and is prepared to meet them on their own ground. With due allowance for Bradford, Feather speaks a competent French and German, as well as a brave burst of Russian, Greek and Italian. Before setting off for Japan, he went to a Chinese restaurant in London and taught himself to eat with chopsticks (to the chagrin of one lot of Japanese trade union hosts who spent a day scouring the town for a knife, fork and spoon). He remembers foreigners' names as fastidiously as he remembers the president and secretary of the Barnsley Trades Council. Between 1958 and 1961 Feather raised £500,000 from the British unions as aid to the unions in developing countries.

Yet none of Feather's many odysseys seems to have had a significant effect on his own thinking. Ernest Bevin's first visit to America, Alan Bullock records in his biography, kindled Bevin's imagination. He came back not only inspired to build Transport House, but full of new ideas about politics and international affairs. Feather returned from his first American trip—a lecture tour in the mid-fifties—proclaiming that "We *do* work harder than Americans". In India, he was angered by the apparent complacency of the trade union leaders, until he learned that their unfamiliar aloofness was a product of their monastic training. In Israel, he showed the Histadrut how to resolve unofficial strikes.

It is partly that Feather's visits are invariably functional. He is restoring or placating the trade union movement; he is a fraternal delegate; he is demonstrating solidarity in South America; he is lecturing or gladhanding; he is investigating overseas information with the Drogheda Committee. Feather seldom has time to stand and stare, or to shed his conceptual shell. He goes abroad with a job to do, and he does it with well-tried tools.

CHAPTER EIGHT

Fifth wheel on the carriage

IF THE FIRST milestone in Victor Feather's advance towards the TUC general secretaryship was his appointment to the organisation department in 1937, the second was his promotion to assistant secretary a decade later. The post was a new one. There was no precedent, and there has been no successor. Walter Citrine had resigned in 1946, first to become a full-time member of the National Coal Board, then chairman of the British Electricity Authority. Vincent Tewson, assistant general secretary since 1931, was elected general secretary in his place.

Tewson recommended the general council to appoint not one but two assistants to work under him. The senior of the pair would be assistant general secretary; the junior would be assistant secretary. Tewson, a man with an orderly mind, was trying to secure the line of promotion. He believed that Edgar Harries, secretary of the organisation department, was planning to retire early, in less than two years. He wanted him as his short-term number two, with George Woodcock, head of research, running himself in as number three. This would leave Feather to take over organisation and gain some experience as a head of department. Before very long, Woodcock would succeed as assistant general secretary and Feather would be established as the next in line.

The two jobs—assistant general secretary and assistant secretary—were advertised. Six candidates, including Harries, Woodcock and Feather, were shortlisted. They were supposed to plump for one or other of the posts, but most (Feather certainly) simply answered: "Either".

When the votes were counted, Woodcock emerged as assistant general secretary and Feather as assistant secretary. There is no record in the general council minutes of how many votes were cast for each candidate, but there seems to have been no doubt about the result. Harries had attracted a pitiful minority. His rejection was doubly painful because seniority is traditionally an asset in the trade union movement. General councillors were not just judging the candidates on their competitive merits, they were consciously passing over the man with the first claim—and passing him over for *two* men who were his juniors. Harries was fifty-eight in 1947 and had served the TUC for nineteen years, for more than half that time as head of the organisation department. Woodcock was forty-two and Feather thirty-eight. Both had been with the TUC for about ten years.

There seems to have been some desultory canvassing of Feather's merits, though he now denies having done any. There is, however, no evidence of either a plot or a campaign. The most convincing explanation of the appointments is that Harries talked himself out of the job —over the years in his relations with members of the general council, and specifically when he was interviewed for it. Harries's ability as an administrator was not in dispute, but his manner was abrupt and sometimes arrogant. He had talked down to members of the general council in a way they would not forget. At his interview he made no attempt to conceal his assumption that the

job was already his. Which committees had he worked
for? Surely, they all knew that. The impression was off-
handed, even sarcastic. The general council was irritated.
Relations between general councillors and members of the
TUC's senior staff are not those of master and man. They
work together and depend on each other. Occasionally,
they drink together (though most general secretaries have
kept their distance). But as senior officers of their own
unions, members of the general council have a strong
sense of rôle. When they are choosing top administrators
their rôle is that of employer. They expect the formalities
to be honoured.

Tewson was surprised and disappointed by the result.
Citrine, who by then had gone to the Coal Board, was
neither. "Edgar Harries always conveyed the impression
of being a cynic," he says. "Now I never had that
impression of him. I knew him, I understood him. He had
one of the clearest brains of anyone I knew. But he was
very caustic in his remarks. They were intended to be
good-natured remarks, but they weren't always understood as that. He would give an impression, too, of
indifference, a lack of depth of earnestness. That was
entirely wrong, but that was the impression he would
convey. A lot of people would get that impression. I
never thought Harries was in the running."

The trouble about the new post of assistant secretary was
that it had no clearly defined functions. There was no
administrative reason for its creation. In Woodcock's
metaphor, it was "the fifth wheel on the carriage".
Feather had found being number two to Harries in the
organisation department instructive, but awkward. Being
number three to Tewson and Woodcock was even more
delicate. "I had to do the jobs Vincent Tewson indicated

I should do, or some jobs that George Woodcock indicated I should do. And since sometimes there was a
difference of opinion, either explicit or implicit, between
Woodcock and Tewson, I found myself in a bit of a cleft
stick from time to time. If I did something that pleased
one, it would be likely to displease the other. It taught me
that I'd got to make my own judgments, to do the job as
well as I could—but whatever it was, whatever difficulty
there was, in the knowledge that I would be criticised
perhaps by either of the other two. Being number three is
much worse than being number two. As number two, you
know you've only got one boss. With number three,
you've got two bosses and neither of them is being very
clear because they always think the other one is giving you
the instructions."

The only specific division of labour between Woodcock
and Feather was over arrangements for the TUC's annual
congress. Woodcock was responsible for the policy side,
Feather for the logistics—the hall, the microphones, the
carafe of water. That apart, the assistant secretary often
got in the hair of his two bosses. He made speeches and
sent copies to the press, which sometimes upset Tewson
and Arthur Deakin, who had succeeded Bevin as leader
of the Transport and General Workers and strong man of
the general council.

Feather cannot bear to be idle. If he cannot find work
to do, he will invent it. But in the late forties and fifties,
there was no need for that. The Communists had come
back from the war more ambitious and better organised
than ever. Feather's old battleground of his trades
council days was ready for the return match.

CHAPTER NINE

In the ring with the Communists

FEATHER'S ANTI-COMMUNISM reaches back to his Bradford youth and the ethical Socialism of the ILP. His teenage politics were sufficiently far Left to worry his father and to enable him to argue with Communists in their own language. But even then Feather recognised the signposts of dictatorship: the rigid discipline, the acceptance of instructions from on high. When he was fifteen or sixteen, he met Saklatvala, the rich Parsee who was Communist MP for Battersea North, and he often attended Communist public meetings. Some of the leaders of the Labour Left tended in the twenties to regard the Communists as a ginger group with a place in the party (Saklatvala won his first election with an official Labour nomination). Feather claims that he was already sceptical. Socialism had to include the fullest freedom of expression. His misgivings were confirmed by what he saw of the Communist-inspired Minority Movement. Feather regarded the organisation as an attempt to establish a parallel, breakaway organisation to the unions. Once again, he could see no sense in trying to further the cause of either the trade unions or Socialism by splitting the Labour movement.

It is part of the mythology of King Street that Feather was once a member of the Communist Party. Feather denies any such idea, but the story is still told. Party officials can produce no evidence from their headquarters files. The industrial department knows all about it, you are told. The industrial department says, "Yes, of course," and cites as its witness Betty Harrison, a retired national organiser of the Tobacco Workers' Union who is a Communist and knew Feather in Bradford. The buck stops there. When I asked Betty Harrison whether she had ever known of Feather's holding a Communist Party card, her answer was an unambiguous "No." When she first knew Feather they were both members of the ILP.

The Communists' postwar offensive in the trade unions began immediately with demobilisation. The trades councils were in the first line of attack. As in the thirties, they were more vulnerable than the national organisations or congress itself. The TUC was sensitive to the danger. Citrine had always insisted on fighting back, and Tewson and Deakin shared his attitude. Woodcock was one of the few in the TUC establishment who had his doubts about the wisdom of such tactics. He believed it was better to leave the Communists alone. With a detachment that owed more to New College, Oxford, than to Smith Square, Westminster, he suggested that it was easy to overestimate what they were doing in King Street. Even in the Electrical Trades Union, the Communist leadership did not have a bad reputation with employers. Woodcock was uneasy, too, about the risk of guilt by association inherent in proscription, even at trades council level. When he had to recommend the expulsion of the ETU years later in his first speech to congress as general secretary, Woodcock deliberately stressed that the union was being penalised not for Communism but for fraud.

Feather would not have disputed this interpretation, but he had none of Woodcock's reservations on the other

Vic Feather playing cricket for TUC *v*. Industrial Correspondents

With Robert Kennedy at Ditchley Park Anglo-American Weekend

scores. He went loyally and vigorously into battle. He drafted two early TUC pamphlets warning the unions and their members of the Communist menace that was upon them. He returned to the trades council circuit, generating resistance. And where necessary he grappled with the enemy.

"There's got to be somebody in the ring," he says. "People are prepared to back you, but they're not prepared to go into the ring. They're not confident enough to fight for themselves. So I got to be in the ring, and the result was that I not only got the spotlight, but I got the pocketful of slush that everybody wanted to throw at me. And it was very largely as a consequence of that that I got the reputation of being a fighter. I wasn't just a gentle sort of fellow who says, 'I've got the ace in my hand, and I'm just going to play it.' I did them the favour of rolling in the mud with them."

Feather was never actually assaulted, though he was jostled often enough and usually jostled back. One man pulled a knife at a meeting, but Feather put that down to natural thuggery rather than dialectical materialism. His fight with the Communists was more like a family quarrel than tribal warfare. The generals were on first-name terms. They understood each other's tactics and techniques. "I knew the Communists very well," Feather smiles, "on the basis of being opponents." "We knew Victor," one of his old foes reflects. "He was the kind of man who caresses your back looking for the right place to put the knife." But family quarrels can be earnest and even gory affairs.

The reasoned tone of Feather's propaganda campaign is caught in *How Do the Communists Work?*, a booklet he wrote for the Batchworth Press in 1953:

G

"Penetration by Communists of existing democratic institutions, and particularly of trade unions, is a high priority Communist Party objective. The aim is to obtain effective control of a democratic organisation and then use it to bring into being a dictatorship. This may seem an impossible task in a country like Britain where Communist Party membership is small, and in great unions where the Communists are in a small—a very small—minority. Yet it can be done. . . . The Communist Party achieved a representation of 40 to 45 per cent on the highest governing body of a union in which only one-half of one per cent of the members were Communists. How is it done? By industrious, guileful and skilful tactics and singlemindedness on the one side, and easy-going apathy on the other."

In the battle for the soul of the trades councils, Feather had one ultimate weapon. The trades councils, which represent all the union branches in a town or district, derive their authority from the TUC. Citrine fostered them as the TUC's local arm, though they never lived up to his aspiration. Their line to the TUC passes through the trades councils joint consultative committee, which has six members of the general council and six elected representatives of the trades councils. The councils have their own conference once a year. If a trades council does not conform to the TUC's "model rules" or refuses to apply congress policy, registration can be withdrawn. The council loses its legitimacy and unions are expected to withdraw their branches.

In practice, this sanction is invoked very sparingly. TUC officials have to prove to the satisfaction of the general council that a trades council is dominated by

Communists (members of a proscribed organisation), or is consistently in opposition to congress policy. Feather found it a difficult card to play. How long was consistent? Eighteen months? Two years? And how could you prove that fellow-travellers were Communists if they did not hold a party card? In 1949, for example, only one trades council—Dagenham—lost its registration. By 1950 it was back in the fold, and one other council was being threatened unless it put its rules in order. In 1951 three councils were banished.

The battle royal reached its climax a year later when the TUC withdrew its fiat from the London Trades Council, the biggest and most powerful of them all. The London Trades Council is unique. It is at once a district federation of local trades councils and a centre for the district committees of individual unions, which affiliate in their own right. It has special status partly because of the special claims of the metropolis, but equally because of its distinctive history. The London Trades Council was founded in 1860, eight years before the TUC itself. George Potter, the militant ideologist of the inaugural TUC, was one of its first officers. Clement Attlee and Herbert Morrison are on its roll of delegates. By 1952, it had an affiliated membership of 800,000 trade unionists. Its main functions were to help unions in distress, raise social issues with the politicians, and organise demonstrations.

Julius Jacobs was elected its secretary in 1945 after years of service as a delegate and executive member. He was a Communist who had never made a secret of his allegiance to the party. Feather, backed by the powerful trio of Arthur Deakin, Tom Williamson of the General and Municipal Workers, and Bob Willis of the London

Typographical Society, soon concluded that the London council was falling into dangerous hands. A number of big unions began withdrawing their district committees, and the TUC gave the council a warning in 1950. Two years later, the TUC withheld its registration.

"The trades councils joint consultative committee have recommended to the general council that they would not be justified in continuing to register the London Trades Council," the report of the 1952 trades councils conference announced. "This council was warned in 1950 that it must act in conformity with the proper functions of trades councils and show positive proof of its willingness and ability to support congress policy. It was also informed it must not allow itself to be used for disruptive propaganda. Since then committees from eight unions have disaffiliated from the trades council through dissatisfaction with its conduct. . . . The council's minutes and report have not revealed significant, positive contributions on either of these points. Indeed the council's proceedings seemed directed to propaganda rather than to achievements. There also appeared to have been collaboration between some of the council's executive and the Communist Party in arrangements for recent demonstrations, although affiliated organisations had not agreed to such collaboration which was contrary to the council's rules."

The trades council fight was superimposed on a backcloth of cold war, "peace" campaigns, and the disintegration along ideological fissures of the World Federation of Trade Unions. Jacobs claims that registration was withdrawn without the London council's foreknowledge. It was notified in March 1952, that its delegates would not be recognised at the annual conference. At that stage, Feather and the TUC were not prepared to discuss their differences further. The London Trades Council records show that in 1952 Jacobs was the only Communist office-holder; but of the twenty-four executive members and officers combined nine were Communists.

The old council refused to go quietly, and 27 of the 50 local trades councils affiliated to it in London and West Middlesex went with it into limbo. The executive even threatened to take the TUC to law. None the less, the TUC formed a new London Trades Council, registered for prudence sake as "London Trades Council (1952)". After a year's defiance, the original council dissolved itself "in the interest of working-class unity". Feather had won, but as a last punch after the bell, the executive solemnly entrusted its historic assets to Julie Jacobs. The assets by then were reduced to the minutes of the London Trades Council from 1860 to 1953. Eighteen years later, the "assets"—in three wrinkled cardboard boxes tied with string—were still in Jacobs's office in King Street. He had doggedly refused to hand them over either to the TUC or to Feather. "I am," he told me, "a law-abiding citizen." But at the end of 1971 Jacobs retired as the Communist Party's assistant industrial organiser, and he discharged his trust by bequeathing the minute books to the care of the TUC general secretary.

This phase of Feather's war with the Communists coincided with the heyday of Senator Joseph McCarthy. In the United States, careers were being destroyed, reputations blackened and friendships poisoned—all ostensibly in the same cause of rooting out the red infiltrators. Yet Feather felt, and still feels, no qualms about his own leading part in the campaign against Communism in the British trade unions. The critical difference for Feather was that here there was no witch-hunt. People were not denounced at a distance or behind their backs. He went in and faced them on the platform. They could, and did, fight back. Feather tried, for instance, to persuade the West Yorkshire Federation of Trades Councils to drop Bert Ramelson from its executive. Ramelson was then a regional organiser for the Communist Party and later became the national industrial organiser, one of the "tightly-knit group of politically motivated men" branded by Harold Wilson with responsibility for the 1966 seamen's strike. But the West Yorkshire federation insisted on keeping Ramelson on its executive, and Feather had to acknowledge defeat. He was, too, bound rather more rigidly by the TUC's version of the Marquis of Queensberry rules than were his opponents, though he was prepared to use the informal channels of Common Cause and Industrial Research and Information Services to reach into union branches. These were *ad hoc* anti-Communist bodies, uninhibited by the protocol of relations between the Labour Party or the TUC on one side and their affiliated unions on the other. Feather was in touch with them, but was not active within them. Their main use to him was as distributing agencies.

Until the mid-fifties, Feather's conflict with the Communists had mostly been open and public. The drama of the second half of that decade took him off the stage and into the prompt box. Feather's contribution to the overthrow of the corrupt Communist leadership of the Electrical Trades Union was unremarked but crucial. All his skills as fixer, propagandist and contact man were extended.

The ETU, one of the big ten British unions, had fallen under Communist control during the Second World War. Jock Byrne, a Glasgow Catholic, tried to break the grip in the early fifties, but without much impact. Allegations of ballot-rigging were first made in the *Daily Telegraph* in January 1956, and were followed in May by an explosive interview with ETU members by Woodrow Wyatt on the BBC television news magazine *Panorama*. At this stage the TUC was reluctant to interfere in the affairs of a member union, and the ETU executive continued to meet all charges with a righteously-offended straight bat. The turning point came towards the end of the year after Russian tanks had suppressed the Hungarian rising. About a third of all card-carrying Communists in Britain resigned or allowed their membership to lapse. They included two leading lights of the ETU, Les Cannon and Frank Chapple. The ex-Communists joined forces with Byrne and brought to the campaign the same singlemindedness and discipline that had marked their Stalinist days.

Every platform of press and broadcasting was exploited, and by the end of 1958 the TUC general council was persuaded to intervene. The ETU was asked for an explanation of its affairs. The prestige and reputation of the trade union movement as a whole was threatened. For nearly two years the general council pressed its demands and the ETU bluffed and prevaricated. In the spring of 1960, the TUC directed the union either to take legal proceedings against those who had 'libelled' its leaders with specific charges of corruption, or to co-operate with the general council in a thorough inquiry. But at this point Byrne and Chapple issued writs of their own against the union and its officers, alleging fraud in the 1959 election for general secretary. Byrne had stood against Frank Haxell, the Communist retiring general secretary, and was declared to have been defeated. The case came before the High Court in 1961, when Mr Justice Winn found that a group of Communist leaders of the union had "conspired together to prevent by fraudulent and unlawful devices the election of the plaintiff Byrne in place of the defendant Haxell as general secretary". The conspirators included Haxell and Frank Foulkes, who had been the ETU's president since 1945. The judge declared Jock Byrne elected forthwith, but Foulkes and his executive remained in office. In September 1961, the ETU was expelled from the TUC. In October, the Labour Party followed suit. Carefully supervised elections in the autumn returned several of Byrne's supporters to the union executive; the Communist grip had finally been broken; and the ETU was readmitted to the respectable ranks of the TUC and Labour Party during 1962.

Feather's first use to the ETU ex-Communists was to open trade union doors that otherwise would have stayed closed. He had known Cannon and Chapple as opponents, and at first was sceptical about their claim to have broken with the Communists. The technique was familiar. Others before them had left the party, insinuated themselves into organisations under more innocent cover, and continued King Street's work. Feather was not easily or quickly convinced, but eventually he accepted Cannon's assurance that their defection was genuine. Once Jock Byrne was satisfied too, Feather was willing to help them. He introduced Cannon and others to shop stewards and branch officials, the sort of people who would invite them to meetings and give them a chance to state their case. These were men who knew and trusted Feather from his years of patiently visiting trades councils—addressing their meetings, presenting their prizes, eating their dinners. If Vic Feather vouched for the ex-Communists, there was no more ground for suspicion.

At the same time, Feather sidled into the propaganda battle. He wrote anonymous articles, briefed other publicists, ghosted revelations. The message was always the same: the Communist leaders were perverting democracy to keep themselves in power. The most resounding article Feather wrote appeared in the *Sunday Times* on 28 February 1960. The heading across three columns read bluntly: "How to Rig a Ballot". It was by-lined "By a Trade Unionist". The author walked a delicate tightrope. He named names and examined methods, but the charges were implied rather than specified. The risks were calculated.

"Mr Foulkes himself probably does not play a direct part in any alleged ballot-rigging or in the manipulations which are said to ensure the victory of Communists to key positions in this union. But Mr Foulkes has been around quite a bit. Although he told his *Panorama* audience last Monday that he did not know of ETU branch secretaries who are Communists, he would probably agree that there are about sixty. The voting figures from most of these sixty branches are always unusually high. The method of voting in the ETU is by secret ballot, so secret in fact that a person who is not an ETU member but who could get hold of a ballot paper could cast a vote without fear of detection. But can that happen?"

The answer, of course, was that it could. And once head office had sent the ballot papers to the branch secretary, here was how:

"The Communist fraction in a branch could go through

the register with the Communist secretary and forward ballot papers only to those whom they knew to be actively interested in the union's work and who might ask questions if they received no papers. As to the balance, what more easy than to destroy some and mark others in favour of the Communist nominee?

"Some of these may be brought to the branch meeting by the shop stewards, all in accordance with rule. Some can be posted to the branch secretary, also in accordance with rule. Then, in full view of the branch meeting, the ballot papers, secret, unnumbered, and unsigned, are counted by the democratically-elected scrutineers. What could be more democratic than that? We will examine any evidence about such jiggery pokery in accordance with the rules, Mr Foulkes and Mr Haxell will say."

It needed only twenty branches out of 650 "fiddling" 100 votes a branch in this way to add a decisive 2,000 votes to the Communist candidate's national total. But a Communist branch secretary might prefer less elaborate means, the article suggested. He might send out all the ballot papers. Perhaps he would receive 100 back. The scrutineers, counting at the branch meeting, would sign the result: 47 votes, say, for the Communist candidate, 53 for his rival.

"Someone, somewhere, somehow, manages to make the Communist vote 147, or even 247; and that is the charge that is sometimes made. The four national scrutineers, headed by Mr Foulkes and Mr Haxell, are not likely to question a return of that kind. The form is all in order so far as they are concerned; it is in accordance with rules. The voting details of all the branches are, of course, published in the executive council minutes, but this is some four or five months after the election and interest has waned. One copy only of these minutes is sent to each branch."

These methods would require the connivance of Communists or fellow travellers in the branch. But branch votes had been rigged, or so it was alleged, without anyone in the branch having the slightest knowledge that it was being done. And here again was our anonymous author to explain how:

"It is the safest possible assumption that, in a branch of 200 members or more, at least 40 will not trouble to vote. The actual number of votes cast may be less than 100. What is to prevent a person posting on different days and at different post boxes in a branch locality 30–40 ballot papers, marked for the Communist candidate, with perhaps two or three marked for the other candidate to give it a realistic look? Ten Communist Party officials covering ten ETU branches each, and arranging for only 30 votes to be posted to each branch secretary, could 'inject' 3,000 votes in the Communist candidate's national total."

The article drew blood because its charges were obviously based on good information. Haxell had just won his election by fewer than 1,000 votes. Foulkes's margin in his last poll had been under 3,000. The author knew the ETU rulebook, and he knew how and by whom it had been drafted. The Communists recognised the hand of an insider, and a friendly journalist in Thomson House confirmed Feather's authorship. It almost cost Feather his career. Foulkes was being pressed by the finance and general purposes committee, the senior policy committee of the TUC general council, to let it investigate the ETU's affairs. He refused to do so because, he said, he had reason to think that one of the officers of the committee had written a defamatory article in the *Sunday Times*. The committee's objectivity was in question.

Feather, who was present, says his neck went hot. If the committee had asked him point-blank, he could not have denied responsibility. For a TUC official to have written such an article in the precarious state of the general council's dialogue with the ETU would have been regarded as a breach of the Ten Commandments. Once the fact was established, Feather would have had to go. And this was at a time when Vincent Tewson was approaching retirement. Feather could expect elevation before long to assistant general secretary. But Foulkes shied away from naming the supposed culprit, and no one else asked the question.

Feather recognised that the best hope of unseating the ETU Communists was Les Cannon. He alone had the tenacity and strength to see the campaign through to a finish. More than most, he had the skill to co-ordinate an elaborate strategy. But times were not easy for Cannon. He had lost his job as head of the ETU educational centre, and was working again at his trade. Simultaneously, Cannon was travelling, speaking, organising. He had little sleep, no family life, and little money to keep his wife and two young sons. Feather's job here—perhaps his most important in the whole campaign—was to sustain Cannon in the fight.

It meant encouraging, reassuring, sometimes cajoling. More to the point, it meant underwriting the Cannon domestic budget. One of Feather's associates outside the Labour movement was David James, Roman Catholic publisher, Antarctic explorer, Eton and Balliol, and Conservative MP for Brighton Kemp Town. They had served together on the Outward Bound trust. Feather went to see him and explained the problem. James agreed to help, and arranged for a group of Catholic business men to pay Cannon a weekly subsistence allowance. It was neither the only nor the biggest outside contribution to the campaign, but it came at a critical moment. The payments continued for about eighteen months. Cannon soldiered on.

CHAPTER TEN

Assistant General Secretary

SINCE THE General Strike in 1926, the TUC has had four general secretaries: Walter Citrine, Vincent Tewson, George Woodcock and Victor Feather. In a variety of permutations, each has worked with all the others. All four attended the TUC's centenary celebrations in 1968. Citrine was active enough to appear on the platform in protest against the Conservative Industrial Relations Bill in January 1971, when he was eighty-three.

Feather's relations with his successive chiefs were as diverse as their personalities and his changing rank. His contact with Citrine from 1937 to 1946 was the least contentious. Citrine was an international figure. Feather was twenty years younger, new to London and to administration. The association was one of junior manager to general manager: admiration on one side, encouragement on the other. Feather likes to compare it to the relationship of baggage man and scorer to the top professional. You travelled in the same party. Sometimes the top professional looked in your direction and smiled. You were able to nod back. You weren't simply one of the crowd who had to keep their distance.

There was nothing cosy about it. Feather never called him "Walter". It was "Sir Walter", and later "Chief" or "Boss". Even when Feather himself was general secretary, he still called Citrine "Chief" when they met. Citrine had no favourites, but he was a demanding boss who gave his subordinates chance to spread their wings and recognised ability when they responded. He was a man of almost boyish enthusiasm, interested in every detail. When he wanted a job doing, his staff dropped everything and did it. If a man did not produce answers immediately, Citrine would be chasing him. Feather, Mr Perpetual Motion 1937, needed no chasing. His loyalty was unquestioning and untroubled.

Citrine, like Feather, was an activist. Tewson was the voice of caution. He was less demanding than Citrine, but just as watchful. He modified, he checked expenditure, he postponed decisions. One of his junior staff was once asked to write an article for the Labour League of Youth on the advantages of trade union membership. His curtain line was: "Nice work if you can get it, and you can get it if you try." The article had to be cleared with Tewson, who frowned his way slowly through the last paragraph. What did that mean, "Nice work if you can get it"? Well, the young man replied, it was a popular song. His readers would understand. Tewson shook his head, crossed out the offending phrases, and wrote in their place: "Suitable employment can be obtained by joining the appropriate trade union."

Feather, number three to Tewson's general secretary, felt frustrated. The brake was always being applied. And things were made no easier by the fact that Tewson's relations with Woodcock, his number two, were often strained. Feather could not walk cheerfully into his room and sit down for a chat. He had to wait to be invited. Feather and Tewson were both Bradfordians, both from the East Ward and its Labour movement. But the sense of kinship was limited—on Feather's side at least. Tewson

was an officer and a gentleman. After joining the army as
a private in 1916, he had risen to brigade staff captain
and was awarded the Military Cross on the Western
Front. After the war Captain Tewson became Bradford's
youngest city councillor, then moved to the TUC in
1925 as the first secretary of its organisation department.
By the time Feather joined the TUC, they were York-
shiremen of a different stamp, the one perhaps too
deliberate, the other too pushing.

George Woodcock's caution was less that of the civil
servant than that of the fatalist. He was eager for change.
"What are we here for?" was one of his first questions to
trade union leaders after he was elected general secretary,
and it was an intellectual challenge he was determined to
press throughout his period of office. But he recognised
that change would come slowly and organically. The
TUC were "the lads in the middle" who had to do "the
best we can". It was a philosophy of evolution and
consensus.

Feather was less willing to wait for eternity. His sights
were set on closer targets. His temperament was less
reflective, his mind less original. As assistant general
secretary, Feather found Woodcock aloof, sometimes
puzzling. Was the general resentfulness directed at him
or at the universe? Did the grunt mean "Yes" or "No"?
Was Woodcock as disdainful of the TUC's organising
side as he often seemed? In the judgment of TUC
veterans who worked with both of them, Woodcock
neglected to exploit Feather's talents as he should have
done. It was not a matter of jealousy, but of failing to
recognise his deputy's capacity for getting things done.

Tension is familiar enough between any office-holder
and his number two. The deputy feels he is not being

With the TUC horse, Manchester 1968

Vic Feather with his wife Alice, son Sandy, and daughter Pat, leaving Buckingham Palace after receiving the CBE, February 1961

allowed his head, even perhaps that he could do the job better. The senior man, in turn, is determined to apply his own ideas, set his own seal on his institution. There was, no doubt, a good deal of this pattern in the uneasy working partnership of Woodcock and Feather. But that was not all. Woodcock was only four years older than his assistant general secretary. He had joined the TUC only a year before Feather, but as a head of department. If Woodcock served his full term, Feather would be over sixty before he could aspire to command. They were contemporaries. They knew each other's strengths and weaknesses. When Woodcock became general secretary and Feather assistant general secretary in 1960, they had worked in the same organisation for twenty-three years. There could be no deference and no distance.

If there was a barrier, it was the barrier of New College. No one ever accused Woodcock of wearing his learning lightly. He had graduated from a Lancashire cotton mill to a first-class degree. His own achievement and his own intellect provided one of the standards by which he judged others. He was a tutor who thought in public, and a very rewarding one for anybody remote and humble enough to enrol. It did not make him an easy chief for a man who had earned the right to consider himself an equal, even if he had earned it in a different school. Feather resented Woodcock's Oxford education not for its own sake, but because of the shell it had left around George Woodcock of Bamber Bridge. He respected his practical knowledge rather than his theorising.

The partnership was, however, not without warmth and occasionally heat. Woodcock was a solitary man who deliberately isolated himself. He sought no friendships on the general council; he kept relations with his staff fairly

H

formal. Woodcock felt closer to Feather than to anyone else at Congress House (even though Len Murray, his successor in research, was another New College economist). He felt that they spoke the same language, had the same background in the ILP. Feather was the only member of his staff who could put his backside on one of Woodcock's chairs, drape his leg over an arm, and say: "Well, George, where are we up to?"

For all his restlessness, Feather knew his place. Woodcock was the general secretary. He was the TUC's spokesman. He made the secretariat's policy. Feather cultivated his own friends, but he did not try to usurp Woodcock's authority. Woodcock valued him as an administrator, and recognised his special interest in organisation, social insurance and the "Ministry of Labour side" (the National Joint Advisory Council that brought together Whitehall, industry and the unions). The general secretary kept his own hand on the reform of union structure, but used Feather's contacts and co-ordinating skills. And whenever there was a major strike, Woodcock would call in his deputy. Although Woodcock sometimes questioned his judgments, Feather would hear things that were useful. He knew the people and he reckoned to know the inner workings of a dispute. Woodcock found him particularly valuable in inter-union conflicts. Feather was more familiar than Woodcock with the collective bargaining map. He could anticipate trouble and make sure that no union that thought it had an interest was left out of consultations. Feather also passed on gossip about the Labour Party—motives, dispositions, actions—though Woodcock affected not to take that too seriously. His dealings were with Ministers, not parties.

During the eight and a half years of their partnership,

Feather made one major excursion into the policy arena. A week before the 1966 congress at Blackpool, Woodcock was taken ill with *angina pectoris* and was ordered to rest. Feather was drafted to make the difficult keynote speech on incomes policy six weeks after the Labour Government had introduced its unpopular July restrictions. Feather was still so little known to the public at large that the newspapers were full of wide-eyed introductory profiles.

"He has been on the staff of the TUC for nearly thirty years," Trevor Evans wrote in the *Daily Express*. "His shrewd Yorkshire perception, his alertness to every undercurrent, his unerring sureness in recognising emerging trends are fortified by a surprising eloquence. He is confident and a master at gauging his audience. . . . He has a deep sense of humour, and by jove he is going to need it."

It was a sensible, even dull speech with none of the Feather flourishes. The cohesion of the Labour movement was on trial as much as the assistant general secretary. In any case, Feather was in no condition for vaudeville. Unknown to all but two or three of his closest colleagues, he was racked with a gastric ulcer.

"Mr Feather's maiden speech met with the great approval of the congress for its workmanlike here-are-the-facts-lads temper," the *Guardian*'s Labour Correspondent commented the next morning. "Nothing could have been in greater contrast to Mr Woodcock's parenthetical thinking aloud style. It was a good deal less fascinating, but possibly more effective for this occasion when delegates had doubts enough of their own without having to follow Mr Woodcock's."

Congress bestowed its reluctant acquiescence on the

Government's pay standstill and the supporting legislation. The margin was only 344,000 in a total vote of 8,800,000. George Woodcock, following the debate at home on television, was content with the result and with Feather's appeal to the strong unions not to use their power selfishly.

A year later Feather played his part in the TUC's resistance to the Labour Government's second Race Relations Bill. This extended the 1965 legislation to cover not only places of public resort, but employment and housing. The union lobby was led by Fred Hayday, chairman of the TUC international committee, with staff work by the international department. Since the preliminary consultations were classified as a Ministry of Labour matter, Feather rather than Woodcock shepherded the deputations.

In retrospect, the campaign looks like a dry run for the industrial relations Battle of Downing Street. The unions were all in favour of giving coloured workers a fair deal, but that was a question of personal relations. Education and persuasion were needed, but the law would only make things worse. Outsiders, most of all lawyers, could not be expected to understand the subtle balances of factory and office life. Feather was worried, too, about the dangers of creating a privileged class of worker. Black men would have a right of appeal against unfair dismissal still denied to white workpeople. That would provoke its own backlash.

Labour Ministers—at the Home Office as well as at the Ministry of Labour—were keen to win the co-operation of both sides of industry. Without it, they knew the law could not be made to work. The result was an honourable draw. Job discrimination was outlawed, but industry was given a first chance to handle complaints.

Only when the voluntary machinery had failed to reach a satisfactory settlement would the Race Relations Board intervene.

The most important trade union merger during the Woodcock years was that between the Boilermakers and Shipwrights in 1963. It brought industrial unionism to the shipyards, which had become a national joke for disputes about which craftsmen were qualified to drill which holes in which raw material. New methods had made the old demarcations meaningless, but the lines were defended down to the last order book. After the 1962 congress, the TUC appointed itself matchmaker and inveigled the two unions around the table. The task of inducing a merger was assigned to Tom Yates, a former chairman of the TUC and leader of the National Union of Seamen, and Victor Feather.

Both unions recognised that amalgamation was essential if they were not to destroy British shipbuilding. But the old suspicions and the old prejudices lingered. Yates and Feather travelled time and again to Newcastle to dispel them. Feather's contribution was to keep the talks going. It was the sort of operation in which he excels: soothing and cajoling, over a drink or over the negotiating table, recognising anxieties, devising formulas. Feather, according to John Dennett, the Shipwrights' assistant general secretary and later vice-president of the amalgamated union, had the knack of remembering incidents in the past when one or other of the unions had come to Congress House with demarcation troubles, and reminding them of forgotten embarrassments.

The matchmaking took a full six months, overcoming differences of personality and trust. In the end Yates and Feather hammered out the terms of an amalgamation resolution to put to both sets of members and compiled a rule book acceptable to both executives. The 100,000 boilermakers and 23,000 shipwrights were led to the altar in September 1963. "Who does what?" became a purely domestic question.

The last full year of George Woodcock's reign, 1968, was the centenary of the TUC. The general council made it an occasion both for watering the trade union roots and for demonstrating that in the 100 years since those earnest craftsmen had assembled in the Mechanics' Institution, David Street, Manchester, their congress had become an estate of the realm.

Feather was appointed impresario. He arranged a day of celebrations in Manchester: a plaque in David Street; a parade of floats and banners, led by the nearest he could get to David Low's white carthorse ("given to remarkable feats of activity, climbing high mountains of recovery, jumping high fences of production and pulling huge loads of export", the cartoonist had once explained on one of his more generous days); a pageant and carnival at Belle Vue, attended by 100,000 trade unionists and their families; Harold Wilson, three brass bands, a male voice choir, primary school dancers from the Lancashire coal-field, beer and fireworks. Harry Mortimer conducted, Gilbert Vinter composed a *Centenary March*.

The week after the anniversary the TUC booked Guildhall and entertained 700 guests, including the Queen and her Ministers, to a banquet. It was the first royal dinner given there by an institution from outside the City. Feather also arranged a concert in the Royal Festival Hall. Sir Adrian Boult conducted the Royal Philharmonic Orchestra and Choir, with Yehudi Menuhin as soloist. Malcolm Arnold composed his *Peterloo Overture* for the occasion and conducted its first performance. The TUC and Hamlyn published a pictorial history, a handsome marriage of 1960s graphics and 1920s nostalgia, that sold 140,000 copies. The BBC made a film, the Post Office printed a commemorative stamp. Feather had his problems with writers and directors, but in the end the point was made in style: the TUC was the people, and the people had arrived.

In reaction against what he regarded as underemployment at Congress House, Feather became treasurer of the London Labour Party in succession to Herbert Morrison in March 1962. The London party was Morrison's creation, a feudal barony that renounced the rule of Transport House. It appointed its own officials and paid its own bills. Feather soon discovered that it also accumulated its own debts. The deficit when he came to office was £1,675 (on a budget of about £11,000) plus a £6,000 mortgage on Herbert Morrison House, the London party's headquarters in Walworth Road south of the Thames. The money had been borrowed from the Amalgamated Society of Woodworkers at 5 per cent interest.

Feather was recruited by the London party chairman, Bob Mellish, to attack the debt, though Mellish acknowledged that the organisation would never be really solvent so long as it insisted on its autonomy. The new treasurer, Mellish testifies, was "an absolute winner at getting money". His appeals to the unions drew an unprecedented response. Feather also increased affiliation fees. Income from this source rose from £744 to £1,245 in his first year. He raised an interest-free loan of £1,000 from the Transport and General Workers and persuaded the

Woodworkers to reduce the rate on their mortgage from 5 to 4 per cent. By the end of 1963, the London party was £443 in surplus and had repaid the Transport and General's £1,000. A year later, the surplus stood at £2,169; and the mortgage was paid off in 1967. Feather resigned in 1968 when the London Labour Party was reconstituted as the Greater London Regional Council of the Labour Party. Transport House took over its finances in good order.

This reversion to political activity need not have been Feather's last. During 1968, after Len Williams had retired to the unlikely haven of the Governor-General's mansion, Mauritius, Feather was sounded for the general secretaryship of the Labour Party. He had been approached for the same post once before. At the end of Morgan Phillips's regime in 1961, a handful of members of the national executive asked Feather whether he would consider being a candidate. They included Barbara Castle and Dai Davies, the steelworkers' leader. There is no reason to think they had the job in their gift. Feather was simply one of a number of possible runners. After establishing that Len Williams, the national agent, was standing, Feather declined to apply. He had not yet come to the end of the road at the TUC.

The 1968 inquiries were more convincing. Feather was sounded separately by both Harold Wilson, the party leader, and George Brown, his discontented deputy. There can be little doubt that had Feather chosen to run, he would have been elected. There was no heir apparent. Sara Barker, the tough little national agent, was retiring in the same year as the general secretary. Since the party constitution precludes a general secretary from sitting in the Commons, there were no willing runners of any weight from the parliamentary party. Harry Nicholas, the eventual choice, was sprung at the last minute with a mighty rubbing of conspiratorial hands by George Brown and James Callaghan. Feather would have been a more acceptable and more appealing alternative.

It was widely assumed at the time that Anthony Greenwood was Wilson's nominee, but the former Prime Minister has consistently denied it. The truth is more devious. I was then the *Guardian*'s Labour Reporter. My beat included the Labour executive. Greenwood's name was floated to me over the lunch table by Richard Clements, the editor of *Tribune*. He claimed to have heard from people close to Wilson that the leader was backing Greenwood for the job. I ought not to write it without checking, he added, but the candidature had its own logic. Greenwood had not been a success at the Ministry of Housing, but loyal old Harold would not find it easy to sack him. And Greenwood was still popular in the constituencies, accepting invitations from all and sundry as assiduously as when he had been a plain MP. Clements admitted rather coyly that Greenwood was also the best man the Left was likely to get for the job, even if his fangs had long ago lost the red of yesteryear.

Like a good reporter, I checked, but alas could dredge no confirmation. Everyone agreed about the logic, but no one else had heard Greenwood's name so much as whispered in the Prime Minister's entourage. Like a good reporter, I was reluctant to lose a story. *Tribune*'s lines did, after all, run deep into the national executive and the parliamentary party. Jennie Lee, Nye Bevan's widow, was that year's party chairman. It was possible that Clements knew something. Eventually I concocted an elaborate and careful paragraph for my paper's *Miscellany* column. It reported rumour with a suitable touch of scepticism, but also pointed the logic. That was the first published mention of Greenwood's name as a possible candidate. His fortunes never looked back until the unhappy July morning when Harry Nicholas pipped him by 14 votes to 12 in the national executive. As soon as the *Miscellany* paragraph appeared, it was taken for granted in Fleet Street that Greenwood was Wilson's man. Eventually, but too late, he probably was. *Tribune* lost a general secretary, but gained a myth.

Feather did not reject the offer without brief consideration. He talked quietly to his friends on the TUC general council and satisfied himself that his succession there was secure. If it was a choice between general secretary of the TUC and general secretary of the Labour Party, he had no doubt which he preferred. Congress House carried more influence. It had been the focus of his ambition for too long to be abandoned now. As it turned out, he had less than a year to wait.

CHAPTER ELEVEN

Outside the walls

VICTOR FEATHER IS a man who cannot say "No". As much by his own choice as by his masters' and comrades', public life has left him little time for private enthusiasms. Although he was teetotal until he was forty, Feather has learned to enjoy good food and good wine. His tastes tend, however, to the wholesome end of the menu (grilled gammon or roast chicken), and he seldom dines out for the sake of it. He smokes cigars, Havana for preference, as an alternative to the fifty Woodbines a day he was warned were bad for his ulcers (which conveniently healed themselves since he had no time for treatment). Sport keeps its appeal. He played cricket on the fringe of the Bradford League and would probably have made that grade but for the demands of Saturday afternoon in the Co-op. In his senior TUC years, though, it has been mostly a snatched hour with *Match of the Day*, or a couple of overs of televised Test before lunch.

For most of his life, he has been a confirmed townsman. No son of the West Riding can be unaware of the countryside. The moors and becks are part of the urban backdrop. But for Feather, the country was a place for weekend schools and ILP outings; the green, brown and purple between meetings. In his fifties he discovered rural England, a landscape with people and animals. It had the force of a conversion, and brought him the nearest he is ever likely to allow himself to relaxation.

In the 1950s and early 1960s, Feather was drawn into the work of Outward Bound and the Civic Trust. He thought they were good ideas and was willing to lend his name and to offer introductions. The Civic Trust in particular wanted to attract Labour and trade union people into its campaign for urban renewal, and Feather was a handy speaker to have in areas like the Potteries or South Wales where a middle-class architect might not have gone down so well. Through the Civic Trust, he met Dora Oxenham, a Labour county councillor from Northamptonshire, an environmentalist before it was fashionable. She was an enthusiast and a great champion of her county. She invited Feather to lunch at her farm and mentioned a derelict thatched cottage not far away. Although there was snow on the ground, Feather went to see it and recognised its potential. It was a ramshackle, overgrown mill beside a silted stream, rusting with corrugated iron and old tin cans. The walls had been fouled by hens; there was no piped water; and the only lavatory was an outside chemical closet. All the same, Feather was attracted and bought the property for £1,200 with an overdraft.

The "thatched cottage" had originally been a flour mill, parts of it dating back to the fourteenth century. In various subsequent incarnations it had been grain store, blacksmith's forge, saw mill and timber yard. The old mill wheel had long since vanished, but there was plenty of scope for the amateur archaeologist. The purchase also embraced the mill house, a rambling two-storey building across the muddy lane, which had been the miller's home, built in instalments during the eighteenth and nineteenth centuries. There were, too, a couple of barns and an acre of paddock and green. The mill stonework and timbers were good, but little else. Feather and his son, Sandy, lately returned from the Merchant Navy, spent £4,000 and much sweat making both houses habitable and clearing the brook. Sandy and his family live permanently in the mill, his parents use the mill house as a weekend retreat.

Northamptonshire was a new world for Feather, even if you could glimpse the Corby steelworks from the hill above the mill house. He could escape from the daily uniform of a suit. The stream became his quiet passion, wading in wellington boots and clutching a shepherd's crook Sandy had bought him in Holborn. There were tiny fish in the water, voles in the banks, and one Sunday he spotted a pair of kingfishers. "You can be on your own there," he says. "You can think a bit and dream a bit." Up the lane there is a wood with badgers, foxes and pheasants; there are fields alive with hares. It is easy to be busy.

While he was serving on the Maud Commission on local government structure (in a fairly passive way), Feather made friends with another member with bucolic interests. The man complained that his ducks were getting too inbred. What he needed was a new drake. Feather offered him one of the flock of ducks and geese Sandy had introduced to the mill stream. A black Muscovy drake with a white band around its throat was dispatched with three females to keep it company. A telegram came by return. It read: "Vicar and harem arrived safely. All performing well." The village post office at Sudborough is still trying to decipher it.

Feather's most lasting extra-mural enthusiasm is for art—first, and hopefully still, as a painter and draughtsman in his own right, but more substantially as a collector. When he was a young man in London, he attended a few classes in oil painting at the St Martin's School of Art; he read up technique in the libraries; and he started visiting galleries to look for the brushmarks.

One day in 1942 he slipped into the Leicester Gallery, then in Leicester Square. One painting, a watercolour by Vanessa Bell, captivated him. The price was £25, and Feather had just been paid about £30 by the BBC for a dozen broadcasts to the West Indies on trade unionism. He went back the next day, and the next. The picture was as enticing as ever, but £25 was a lot of money and Feather put temptation behind him. He would go to see it once more on the exhibition's last day. With luck it would have been sold. In fact Feather arrived at five past one and the "Closed" sign was already out. Like a diffident swain, he pushed the door and found it unlocked. The watercolour was still there, and Feather bought it. He knew nothing of the painter or of Bloomsbury, and had to ask before discovering that Vanessa Bell was Virginia Woolf's sister and Clive Bell's wife.

This was the almost accidental beginning to a collection that ran to sixty paintings or pieces of sculpture when Feather took over the general secretary's office at Congress House. He buys things he likes, mostly by young artists. He is not shy of professional advice, but never resells for profit. His dearest purchases were two pieces by Jacob Epstein—one a bronze of Paul Robeson, which cost him £150 he had been saving for a second-hand car; the other a head of Epstein's granddaughter, for which he paid £250. Feather has, too, some drawings by Frank Dobson and C. W. R. Nevinson. His office, which looks like a gallery between shows with pictures stacked everywhere, is dominated by a muscular, stainless steel hermaphrodite by James Butler and a calm, boyish head by Robert Mitchell. But perhaps the pride of the Feather collection is a pair of forged Constable landscapes, which he bought for £20 each at West End sales. "They're quite nice pictures," he says, "and I'm glad to have them. The National Gallery said I'd probably get thirty quid for the frames, but I couldn't bear to sell."

Victor Feather, patron of the arts, and Victor Feather, organisation man, overlapped in 1960 when Arnold Wesker was flighting his ideas for Centre 42. Without Feather's help, Wesker says, the project would hardly have got off the ground. Wesker had given a lecture at Oxford, criticising the Labour movement for neglecting the artist in society. A copy of his lecture was sent to every trade union, with a proposal that the TUC should inquire into the state of the arts. The (limited) result was Resolution 42, submitted by the Cinematograph, Television and Allied Technicians, to the 1960 congress at Douglas.

Wesker went to lobby, but knew almost nobody there. A sympathetic journalist pointed to a room full of pressmen and union general secretaries. That was where he ought to be. The reporter told him to wait and went in. "Out of the shadows," Wesker says, "a man came and thrust a yellow ticket into my hand and said: 'I think that's what you want, lad. Go in there and do your damnedest.'" Open Sesame.

The man was Feather, whom Wesker had never even heard of at that time. As hopes and ideas for engaging the Labour movement in the arts developed, Feather became a benevolent uncle: meeting the playwright's family, going home with him to Highgate for dinner, showing Wesker his pictures. The rift came when Wesker did not turn enough to Feather. Wesker was anxious to preserve Centre 42's independence. Eventually, Feather was instructed by the general council to tell Wesker that Centre 42 should feel no obligation to the TUC, but that equally the TUC would feel no continuing obligation to him. It was an unhappy end, both to a friendship and to one of the props that might have sustained a brave idea.

Without bitterness, the playwright modelled Brian Cambridge, one of the characters in *Their Very Own and Golden City*, on Feather. The echoes are obvious. Cambridge, a wise and practical old hand, is trying to find a compromise between Andy, the visionary who wants the unions to finance industry for his utopian cities, and the hard-faced men of the general council, Ted Worthington and Bill Matheson:

> CAMBRIDGE: For the last three years the general council have advised congress not to vote in favour of financing industry in the six cities. Now I'm not saying the general council would ever recommend congress to finance even one city, but it's bloody certain they can't consider six. If you want the scheme to make sense at all, then drop the other five.
> ANDY: Drop them?
> WORTHINGTON: Drop them, Andy, drop them. Build one of your cities and change the resolution accordingly. You don't stand a snowball's chance in hell of getting congress to vote money for six. . . .
> ANDY: Can you guarantee they'll decide to recommend the financing of industry in one city?
> CAMBRIDGE: Andy, lad, for Christ's sake. You know I can't guarantee a thing like that.
> ANDY: I'm really being pushed to the wall, aren't I?
> CAMBRIDGE: I'd say you were being given a way out. You've now got the possibility of making one city work; before, there was the possibility of nowt. Think on it.

Vic Feather, countryman, relaxing in Northamptonshire

... BUT WHAT HAPPENS WHEN YOU GET BACK TO THE PLACE FROM WHICH YOU FIRST STARTED SAID ALICE.

Cartoon by Richard Willson dated 25 May 1969

CHAPTER TWELVE

The Battle of Barbara's Bill

IT IS NOTHING new for a general secretary of the Trades
Union Congress to earn his commission on the field.
Walter Citrine was still acting general secretary when he
guided the workers of Britain through the General Strike
in 1926, but his succession and authority were less secure
than Victor Feather's in the spring of 1969. Citrine was
thirty-eight and had still to prove his stature. The TUC
headquarters staff, which he had controlled since the death
of Fred Bramley in 1925, was very small, its influence
limited. The general council was already dominated by
Ernest Bevin.

In contrast, Feather was sixty-one when he led the
TUC through the Battle of Barbara Castle's Industrial
Relations Bill. His strengths were recognised by the
union leaders, who regarded him as one of their peers. He
had served the TUC for more than thirty years. His
instincts were its instincts, and he was equipped to
anticipate its judgments and interpret its mind. The
institution had grown in scale and command. It would
have been harder than ever to import a general secretary
from outside Congress House, and there was no rival of
comparable weight inside. Feather was confident that
congress would elect him come September. At the suggestion of Frank Cousins, the general council underlined
the point by raising Feather's salary to full general

secretary's level immediately after he took over from George Woodcock on 1 March.

Feather marched into Downing Street uninhibited by reservations about his professional future, or about his right to speak for the unions. John Newton, that year's TUC chairman, was content with a supportive rôle. He is an easygoing Yorkshireman, a bachelor who spends his spare time painting landscapes and composing meticulous and unpublished verse dramas. Newton was born within three months and ten miles of Feather, and was proud of their affinity. The chairman's job, as he saw it, was to ensure unanimity in the general council and to flap the towel, soak the sponge and dispense wisdom in Nipper Feather's corner.

Trade union leaders suspected from the start that penal sanctions against strikers were thrust on Ray Gunter and then Barbara Castle by their officials. They found confirmation as early as November 1965, when the Ministry of Labour suggested to the Donovan Commission on trade unions and employers' associations that "a most promising change in the law might be to make procedural agreements for settling disputes legally enforceable". The submission was not that of the Minister, but that of the Department. It was presented by the Permanent Secretary, Sir James Dunnett. The declared object was to make the unions reform their internal organisation and take disciplinary action against unofficial strikers, who accounted for 90–95 per cent of all stoppages in British industry.

Donovan rejected this view. His report, published in June 1968, was many things to many men, but the balance of its argument was that the Government would be better treating the disease than the symptoms. Britain, it said,

had two systems of industrial relations. One was the formal
system, with national agreements negotiated between
unions and employers. The other was the informal system
of bargaining within the factory for such industrial staples
as piecework, incentive and overtime payments.

"The bargaining which takes place within factories,"
Donovan found, "is largely outside the control of employers' associations and trade unions. It usually takes
place piecemeal and results in competitive sectional wage
adjustments and chaotic pay structures. Unwritten
understandings and 'custom and practice' predominate.
These developments help to explain why resort to unofficial and unconstitutional strikes and other forms of
workshop pressure has been increasing." What Donovan
proposed was that this informal system should be recognised and regularised. Boards of directors should accept
their responsibilities and negotiate company industrial
relations agreements. These would have to be registered,
and a new Industrial Relations Commission should be set
up to supervise them.

George Woodcock was a member of the Donovan Commission, and the report reflected his outlook as well as that
of Hugh Clegg, an assertive and skilful professor of
industrial relations. It was coolly received by Harold
Wilson's Government. Whether or not—as most union
leaders and industrial correspondents believed—the
Labour Ministers had appointed the commission to give
them a respectable excuse for bashing the unions, Donovan's slower and subtler prescription was politically
unpalatable. By the end of 1968 Barbara Castle, who had
replaced Ray Gunter in St James's Square and assumed
the resounding title of First Secretary and Secretary of
State for Employment and Productivity, had convinced

herself and the Prime Minister that unofficial strikes must
be outlawed.

The Conservatives had anticipated Donovan and
published their own industrial relations programme, *Fair
Deal at Work*, in April. It proposed a sixty-day cooling-off
period before certain stoppages; compulsory secret strike
ballots; the removal of legal protection from unions
engaging in demarcation strikes or strikes to enforce a
closed shop; and to make agreements legally binding
except when employers and unions agreed otherwise. At
the beginning of December Edward Heath threw down
the Conservative challenge: Why was the Labour Government delaying its own plans for dealing with strikes? Was
it afraid to tame the unions?

The Tory campaign coincided with just the sort of
dispute that had angered the public and embarrassed
British governments in the banks and chancelleries of the
world. Twenty-two machine setters at the Girling brake
factory in Bromsgrove, Cheshire, had walked out because
a member of the "wrong union" had turned an oil supply
valve. As a result more than 5,000 car workers were laid
off at other plants.

The Girling strike was the last straw, but as Peter
Jenkins puts it in his racy reconstruction, *The Battle of
Downing Street*, "The problem of doing something about
industrial relations became interwoven with Harold
Wilson's problem of how to restore the authority of his
Government and his own authority as Prime Minister."
Public opinion polls were swinging violently against
Labour and its leader. A Gallup poll published in the
Daily Telegraph on 13 December registered only 30 per
cent of the electorate willing to vote for the Government.
A mere 17 per cent approved of its record. No more than

18 per cent expected its economic policies to succeed.

At the end of November, in the eye of an international monetary crisis, Roy Jenkins introduced his second "mini-Budget" of the year. Two weeks later, on 6 December, the City of London went berserk. With more than usual justification, Wilson dubs it "Mad Friday" in his personal record of the Labour Government. Rumours of Ministerial quarrels and imminent dissolution of Parliament were rife. It was even whispered that another devaluation was on the way. Phantom resignations flew in all directions. Abdication was not ruled out. Sober denials from Downing Street and Buckingham Palace made no difference, and by the end of the day Britain had lost $100 million of its reserves. It was damaging and pathetic, but the message of Mad Friday was that public confidence in the Government's management of the economy had slumped so low that even the wildest rumour had its takers.

Something had to be done. Reform of industrial relations was on the agenda. Barbara Castle and her officials had their plans ready. Time was running out for the vacillating unions and the impotent Confederation of British Industry. The Labour Government would be demonstrating both its capacity for action and its independence of its traditional sectional interest, the trade unions.

If the Government's first mistake was to disavow Donovan, its second was to rush its fences with the TUC. Barbara Castle invited George Woodcock to St James's Square and gave him a private glimpse of her draft White Paper. She had Wilson's consent, though the Cabinet had not yet seen her proposals. The Minister and her senior officials took the TUC general secretary to be reacting favourably to the plan. "I don't think there is anything in this to which the unions can fundamentally object," he was monitored as muttering. Woodcock's own version is significantly different. As he remembers it, his response was: "There's nothing here that surprises me." After the Government's grudging welcome to the Donovan Report, world-weary George was hardly astonished that it was going to introduce penal sanctions against unofficial strikers.

Whether Woodcock was more precise in retrospect than he was at the time, or whether Barbara Castle heard what she wanted to hear, is immaterial. The Minister was impressed with what she thought he said, and accepted the general secretary's advice to discuss the document with the general council. She knew she was risking a leak to the press, but was ready to take a chance in the interest of good will. In the event, she had underestimated the vehemence of trade union hostility—and simultaneously alienated Cabinet colleagues who resented learning about a major and sensitive piece of government policy courtesy Fleet Street and the general council of the TUC. Wilson acknowledges the error in his book on the Labour administration. Richard Crossman, he records, wrote to him after the battle was over saying that one of the great difficulties for some members of the Cabinet sprang from the fact that the scheme became public knowledge before the Cabinet could express a view on it. "He was right," Wilson confesses.

Apart from the Prime Minister, Barbara Castle's strongest ally at this stage was Roy Jenkins. The Chancellor had seen her proposals before they were laid in front of the Cabinet as a whole. He was in full agreement with her general approach. When the Cabinet discussed a timetable in January, Jenkins pressed for quick legislation. He was ready for trouble and thought it wise not to court an angry debate at the party conference in October. Jenkins argued, too, that they should not let the issue drag into the last session of the 1966 Parliament. Contentious measures are not the thing for a pre-election year.

Barbara Castle took the opposite tack. Evidently she still nursed hopes of winning over the unions. Her White Paper, *In Place of Strife*, published on 17 January, was a "blueprint for the reform of collective bargaining". It was designed as a balanced package of rights and obligations for the unions. Only three of the twenty-seven proposals involved any use of penal powers. These were: a compulsory twenty-eight-day cooling-off period in certain strikes; enforced ballots before some official strikes; and imposed solutions as a last resort in inter-union disputes. The Cabinet division over timing was clear, but not particularly bitter. The Prime Minister supported Barbara Castle, and the Employment Secretary's slower strategy carried the day.

Towards the middle of March, however, Wilson and Castle changed their opinions. Jack Jones, the new but not quite crowned leader of the Transport and General Workers, had started reminding his union's sponsored MPs of their obligations. The shadow of a party conference like those Hugh Gaitskell endured on public ownership and nuclear disarmament deepened. Like Macbeth spurred by his rapacious lady, Wilson decided that it would be better done quickly. Roy Jenkins needed no persuasion to announce the legislation in his Budget speech on 15 April. There were precedents of a kind.

The 1968 Budget speech had included a major statement by Jenkins on prices and incomes policy. Besides, the Chancellor had already agreed to announce the end of the current phase of prices and incomes restraint in his 1969 Budget speech. This was a concession to the unions and other Labour critics, and Jenkins was anxious to have something to balance it. The foreign bankers were still looking over his shoulder. British investors still needed reassurance. Jenkins believed that a Bill was possible in what remained of the 1968–69 session. The longer they waited the harder it would become.

The Battle of Barbara's Bill became Victor Feather's battle on 1 March when George Woodcock resigned from the TUC to become the first chairman of the Commission on Industrial Relations. Feather is a machine politician, a scarred and decorated hero of the smoke-filled room and the midnight formula. He is, too, a son of the Labour movement, old enough to have been influenced by the shock of 1931. In the spring of 1969, he was fighting to preserve his and the unions' industrial way of life. Equally, he was fighting to save the unity of the movement from the folly of its leader.

At the same time, Feather privately hoped that the threat of legislation would be a goad for the unions. Feather wanted the TUC to become more involved in industrial relations. Traditionally, the unions had insisted that relations with employers—negotiations, agreements, tactics—were their own affair. Congress House had to be informed when there was to be a stoppage, but only because that was in the rules. The TUC was expected to keep its distance, unless it was called in to conciliate when the strike had run its course. Feather had been restive under George Woodcock. He had wanted more active and earlier intervention by the TUC, but felt rebuffed. Now he was the acting general secretary, no longer shackled by his own conviction that organisations collapse if the number two pursues a line contrary to his chief's. Feather needed no instruction from the politicians on the damage that could be done by inter-union and unofficial strikes. He was certain that the law was not the answer, but the distant crackle of court summonses might drive the unions his way. It was one more good reason for keeping the line open between Bloomsbury and Downing Street.

Feather never forgot, however, that he was the servant and spokesman of the general council. He kept John Newton informed of his private meetings with Harold Wilson and Barbara Castle. He was keen to help the Government towards a compromise (short of acquiescing in penal sanctions), but was no less fastidious about preserving the TUC's independence. As he saw things, Feather was acting in the interest of the trade union movement. He knew and sensed the attitudes of the general councillors. There could be no question of pulling the wool over their eyes, or of leading them down paths they would refuse to tread.

Although Feather has often billed himself as the most political general secretary in the TUC's history, he deliberately kept the Labour Party at arm's length for the duration of his war with the Prime Minister. He had no contact with the trade union group of Labour MPs. The only politician he discussed events with outside the Downing Street dialogue was Douglas Houghton, the respected chairman of the Parliamentary Labour Party, who had been both a Cabinet Minister and for seven years in the 1950s a member of the TUC general council. Even then, the first meeting between Houghton and Feather did not take place until May, four months after the publication of *In Place of Strife* and a month after Roy Jenkins had announced early legislation. The approach came from Houghton, and Feather was glad to see him on TUC ground.

On Sunday 11 May, Feather shared a platform with Wilson at the fiftieth anniversary conference of the Union of Post Office Workers. He had learned only on the Saturday when he was travelling to Bournemouth with John Newton that the Prime Minister was planning a speech on industrial relations. Feather spent most of Saturday night and Sunday morning drafting his counter. "The TUC," he said in a line that most reports picked out, "has no hand or part in any political shenanigans at Westminster or anywhere else." The temptation had been more specific than any of his listeners guessed.

Westminster was jangling with plots and rumours of plots. The TUC had no trouble keeping out. The politicians were sharpening their own axes for their own reasons, but Feather was the acting general secretary of the TUC negotiating with a government on a matter of industrial relations policy. It could have been a Tory Cabinet as easily as a Labour one. That, at least, was how Feather chose to play his hand. He received one direct approach. A discontented and senior ex-Minister suggested that he and Feather should team up with the Labour general secretary, Harry Nicholas, and launch a campaign to remove Harold Wilson from the leadership. There is no reason to think that Nicholas knew anything about either the approach or the proposition. Feather rejected the idea out of hand, refusing even to discuss it with the ex-Minister.

Barbara Castle, for one, appreciated Feather's scruples in staying out of the Westminster cockpit. But the acting general secretary was not unaware of what was happening in the parliamentary party. Labour MPs could be left to get on with it. Fifty-seven of them voted against the Government on 3 March when the Commons debated *In Place of Strife*, and another thirty abstained. Of the four elected officers of the parliamentary party—the chairman and his three vice-chairmen—only one voted with the Government. By the end of the month, even the loyal vice-chairman, Will Howie, a former Government Whip, had changed sides. Ray Gunter, who had returned to the back benches after a reluctant stint as Minister of Power, abandoned his broad support for his successor's policy. "I see no hope," he intoned, "of the Labour Party winning the next election, certainly not under its present leadership." With a handful of early exceptions, the trade union group—127 MPs sponsored by 25 unions—was consistently unhappy with the Government's proposals. So, predictably, were the habitual rebels of the smaller *Tribune* group. By mid-May an action group led by Eric Moonman, an earnest middle-of-the-road MP of recent vintage, was brandishing a list of sixty-one kindred souls pledged to vote against the Bill and thirteen more to abstain.

Douglas Houghton completed the jigsaw at a meeting of the Parliamentary Labour Party on 7 May. "We want something in place of strife in our own party," he said. "No good can possibly come of any clash or split within our movement. No good that any contentious Bill of this kind can do to industrial relations or the economy will redeem the harm we can do to our Government by the disintegration or defeat of the Labour Party. . . . We are still the Government. We still have the power to influence events our way. But the best hope of all is in a united party, here and outside. The Government and the party are one, and the sooner we become indivisible the better. Ministers must not fall into the error that their determination and their resolve to force things through the party and through Parliament is either desirable or possible. It can only be done with us, it cannot be done without us. We must all strive to prevent government by disintegration of the Labour Party—there is no future in that for anybody, least of all for industrial relations."

Houghton's statement from the chair was distributed to the press and was immediately trumpeted as a challenge to Wilson's leadership. As Houghton himself was quick to explain, that was not its intention. It was, though, an important and public warning. In Peter Jenkins's phrase, Houghton was "declaring the backbenchers' dispute with the Government official".

Against this known background, Feather was confident that he could head off legislation. A Labour Government could not rule in a vacuum. It needed the support of its MPs and its executive, and both were seriously in doubt. Wilson was trying to go pontoon with a three and a two. Feather was conscious, too, of the strength of his own position. He had the solid backing of the whole trade union movement and an almost unanimous general council. The unions dominated the Labour Party conference and were its principal source of funds. The TUC held an ace and a king.

None the less, in his gloomier moments Feather was worried that the unions would become so disillusioned not only with the Labour Government, but with the Labour Party, that they would disaffiliate. His nightmare was of a rift between the political and industrial wings of the movement transcending even 1931.

Feather's strategy, therefore, was intricate and—on the surface—not always consistent. His first aim was to stop the Government legislating for fines on strikers. The duel would be hard, but in the end he expected to win. But he had to beware of inflicting mortal wounds. To destroy the Labour Government would only let in the Tories—and *their* legislation would be much more difficult to resist. To kill the Labour movement would be to kill himself.

It was the kind of labyrinth in which British trade union officials thrive. They are used to fighting limited wars. Unconditional surrender is never the objective. Their concern is for wages not revolutions. They have too big a stake in the survival of their industries—and their members' jobs—to put them at ultimate risk. Union leaders are bred for compromise, but on the best conceivable terms they can screw out of the employers. The weapons are aggressive and devious. Stamina is essential. The skill is to know when to settle, then to save your adversary's face. But the battles are real, and so is the blood.

Politicians are more accustomed to war games than to wars. The party Whips march their men in and out of the lobbies like the Grand Old Duke of York's compliant ten thousand. There are few crises, and Governments generally come through. Plots and counter-plots seldom pierce the skin. The ambitious project themselves and their talents. Disaffected backbenchers sign melancholy motions in the tea room. Ministers agitate and horse-trade, for parliamentary time and Treasury money. When they do fight, it tends to be for identifiable prizes: a seat in the Commons, the key to No. 10, an Act on the Statute

Book. The winners know they have won, the losers know
they have lost.

Harold Wilson is no frail dilettante. He can wheel and
deal with the best, puffing smoke signals and shaking the
big stick of party leadership. But he has little appetite for
confrontation. The more his match with the TUC became
an argument about the terms of a compromise, the more
the general council was playing on home ground. Nevertheless, it took eight full meetings around the Downing
Street table, five limited sessions, and up to a dozen
informal chats between the Prime Minister and Victor
Feather between 11 April and 18 June, before they
settled. The union leaders found Barbara Castle more
stubborn than Wilson. It was, after all, *her* policy, which
she was prosecuting with the unique intensity of conviction she brings to everything she undertakes, from
overseas development to restoring antique brassware.
Wilson insists in his book, however, that "at every stage
in the discussions I was at least as demanding as she
was".

At first the argument was ostensibly about whether the
Government would go through with legislation in the
1968–69 session. The general council met Barbara Castle
four days after she had published *In Place of Strife*, and
believed that they had agreed on a timetable of consultation. As the TUC understood it, there would be a major
Bill in November, early in the *next* session. Discussion of
the White Paper's twenty-seven proposals would continue
till the end of May, after which the parliamentary drafts-
men could get to work on their complicated text. Instead,
in the week before the Budget, the political correspondents
began speculating on a short, early Bill incorporating the

penal sanctions. Trade union ears started twitching.

Ministers had indeed decided that Roy Jenkins would announce both the end of compulsory restraint on prices and incomes and the Industrial Relations Bill. Wilson was booked to meet the TUC on the morning of Budget Day to hear formal representations on Barbara Castle's White Paper, but now decided it would be better to see union leaders earlier. The finance and general purposes committee went to No. 10 on 11 April, the Friday morning before the Budget. This first meeting left a sour taste, which lingered in union mouths for most of the next two months.

The TUC nailed its banner to Donovan. Real progress could be made on major reform of collective bargaining. The law had no place in industrial relations, and anyway it would not work without TUC co-operation. The Prime Minister doffed his cap at Donovan, too, but insisted that the public wanted action against "unofficial strikers who bring about industrial anarchy". Action had to be taken by industry and Government, but there was no time to leave the matter entirely in the hands of industry. And the November timetable? Well, Wilson said, the Government was "not necessarily" committed to it. The Cabinet would have to consider the position in the light of the TUC's comments.

The following Tuesday, after four more days of increasingly confident press prophecy, the short Bill was announced. The union leaders felt they had been hoodwinked. The decision could not have been made overnight. Their bitterness was reflected in a speech John Newton delivered to the Scottish TUC at Rothesay a few hours before the Chancellor unveiled his Budget.

"The attitude of the Government to the trade union

movement," the TUC chairman said, "is now inexcusable. I was the chairman of the TUC delegation which met the Prime Minister last Friday, and I got the impression when I read the press on Saturday morning regarding that meeting that the Prime Minister was more concerned with provocative political propaganda than sober consultation. Mr Wilson said that the Government had not made up its mind on the timing of the legislation. It could be the end of this parliamentary session or during the next. At no time did he say that legislation was imminent. However, if press reports this morning are correct that yesterday the Cabinet decided to introduce anti-strike legislation in this session, the question has to be asked: Did the Cabinet persuade the Prime Minister of the urgency of legislation or did the Prime Minister persuade the Cabinet? The trustworthiness of the Prime Minister himself now depends on the answer to that question."

This sense of being patronised and deceived persisted on the trade union side. At a later Downing Street meeting a plate of ham sandwiches had been put out for the general council. By the time the TUC team had left the Prime Minister, the sandwiches were dry and curling at the edges. Albert Martin, the earthy little leader of the Nottinghamshire miners, took Victor Feather by the arm and mumbled: "Even the sandwiches are sneering at us."

All the same, a useful seed had been sown at the first, pre-Budget meeting. Picking up a hint from Feather, the Prime Minister said that if the TUC wanted the Government to withdraw its proposals, the unions would have to produce an alternative plan which was "equally as urgent and equally as effective" as the Government's would be. It was a point Wilson repeated frequently during the next

Trafalgar Square demonstration February 1971

Vic Feather leading
Tom Jackson across the
plinth in Trafalgar
Square during the post-
men's strike, 1971

nine weeks—in his meetings with the TUC and with Labour critics. Feather had deliberately cut the Prime Minister an escape hatch. He wanted to save a Labour Government (preferably, but not necessarily, under Harold Wilson). He also wanted to sharpen the TUC's power to intervene in industrial relations.

The legislation was announced by Roy Jenkins on 15 April. Barbara Castle revealed the details the following day:

1. All workers would have a statutory right to belong to a trade union;

2. Unions would have an enforceable right to recognition where there was no inter-union dispute;

3. If the TUC could not resolve inter-union disputes, the Employment Secretary would be empowered to enforce a solution recommended by the Commission on Industrial Relations;

4. The Employment Secretary would be empowered to order a twenty-eight-day conciliation pause in unconstitutional stoppages, and would also be able to order a return to the *status quo* while negotiations continued;

5. Workers laid off because of a strike in which they were not directly involved would be able to receive unemployment benefit.

Compulsory strike ballots had been dropped, but of the five main provisions numbers three and four stuck in union gizzards. Both were backed by the threat of fines for a breach of Government order. Ministers were anxious to dispel any talk of prison. The fines would be civil debts and collected as such. But what if workers or unions refused to pay? It was suggested that an offender's goods could be seized, or that the fine could be deducted from his pay packet. Whatever the Ministers said, they knew as

K

well as the TUC that the last resort would be either to send recalcitrants to prison or to make an ass of the law.

When the finance and general purposes committee met the Prime Minister and Employment Secretary immediately after Barbara Castle's statement, it quickly emphasised that the question of how fines were enforced was a minor one. The trade union movement was "unalterably opposed" to the use of fines. Once fines were introduced into industrial relations, it would be possible to widen their use in future. And the restoration of the *status quo* in an unofficial dispute (even if it meant that the strikers' position would not be weakened by a return to work) would in no way diminish the sense of grievance if financial penalties were imposed. In Victor Feather's words, the TUC would not accept the introduction of a "taint of criminality" into industrial relations. Barbara Castle's mixture may have been laced with treacle, but the unions were having none of it.

Between 16 April and 12 May, when the general council presented the Government with its alternative *Programme for Action*, Feather had at least three private sessions with the Prime Minister. The acting general secretary went to dinner at Downing Street on 9 May. Barbara Castle was also there. Earlier that day, the Cabinet had met jointly with the Labour national executive. James Callaghan had made a speech disassociating himself from Cabinet policy on industrial relations. For this or other reasons, Barbara Castle was sulky and angry at the dinner table. She and Feather were at each other's jugulars. It was all or nothing, with much muttering into the soup and no trace of Yorkshire camaraderie. Somehow, Feather managed to convey to Wilson that he was making progress with the TUC. The

Prime Minister told him in return that the Government had decided to defer introduction of the Bill until after the TUC had held a special congress at Croydon on 5 June.

The full general council—all thirty-nine members—followed Feather back into No. 10 on 12 May to present the TUC programme. Harold Wilson recorded in his diary that the meeting was "markedly friendly and comradely". He sensed a strong desire by the union leaders to avert a split in the Labour movement. No doubt that was so, but on the specific issue of fining unofficial strikers harsher emotions show through the Dettol of the TUC minutes, published later that year in the general council's annual report to congress:

"The TUC were not trading sanctions with the Government. Unions and union members generally accepted the judgment of their peers, and threats of automatic sanctions would be self-defeating. There could not be precision in this area: flexibility was the key to useful action in attempting to bring order and method to industrial relations problems. . . . The general council's approach was not to impose sanctions at every turn but to deal with every situation on its merits. The major fallacy of the Government's thinking was the belief that the imposition of automatic sanctions would solve disputes."

Flexibility is the key. If Victor Feather is ever elevated to the peerage, he will set it in lights on the family escutcheon. But it was not good enough for the politicians. Barbara Castle's repeated and specific question was: "What will you do?" The unions had dallied long enough, and the unofficial strikes continued. The Government had a clear-cut answer. Where was the TUC's? What were the unions prepared to do to ensure that their members returned to and remained at work during negotiations? Without a clearer definition, the general council's proposal for dealing with such disputes "could at best be regarded as a pious hope". The Ministers wanted the TUC to use its rules to enforce a return to work. The unions were not playing.

Their *Programme for Action* showed, however, that they were prepared to act crisply on inter-union disputes. The unions proposed to give Congress House new powers to intervene in any dispute arising from demarcation or other inter-union problems. The general council would be able to make binding awards. If an individual union refused to accept an award, the general council would be free to suspend it from membership or to report it to congress with a view to disaffiliation. Barbara Castle's judgment, rapidly endorsed by the Prime Minister, was that the TUC had moved "farther and faster in the previous two weeks than in all the past forty years", and it had moved because the Government was threatening it with legislation. All the unions had accepted this proposal, which effectively removed inter-union disputes from the Downing Street battlefield.

At its next session, on 15 May, the general council tried to meet the Government if not half way then at least quarter way on unofficial strikes. *Programme for Action* proposed an extension of congress Rule 11, which authorises the TUC to intervene in disputes threatening the jobs of workers whose unions are not directly involved. Unconstitutional stoppages were to be brought within the scope of this rule. The TUC would be able to investigate a dispute and make recommendations.

"The general council are confident," a revised version of the TUC programme said, "that, in the case of unofficial and unconstitutional strikes, unions will impress on their members the advantages to be gained from accepting TUC assistance in settling the dispute and will accept responsibility for doing everything within their power to ensure that their members accept recommendations by the TUC.

"The general council would also require unions to satisfy them that they had done all that they could reasonably be expected to do to secure compliance with a recommendation (or an award, where this has been made), including taking action within their own rules if necessary. The general council also consider that it should be made clear in Rule 11 (as is already implicit in that rule, and as is explicit in Rule 12) that in the unlikely event of a union refusing to abide by a decision of the TUC the general council can take action under Rule 13."

Rule 12 is the one dealing with inter-union disputes, which the TUC had already agreed to amend. Rule 13 covers the "conduct of affiliated organisations". It empowers the general council to suspend a union disobeying TUC directions and to report it to congress with a view to disaffiliation. The main amendment in the TUC's draft programme was to substitute the word "require" for "expect". Unions would now be required to satisfy Congress House that they had done all they could to secure compliance with a TUC recommendation.

There was, as Feather acknowledged, nothing very new in the revised version. When he showed it informally to Wilson, the Prime Minister recognised it as "a big move forward, but not enough". There was still no follow-through, no union guarantee to use every penalty to enforce compliance with a TUC call for a return to work. It was, though, as Wilson noted rather ominously, well drafted. Even if it did not convince the Government or the electorate, it would convince many trade union group MPs that the TUC meant business. For the first time, Feather also told Wilson that the general council demanded the abandonment of penal clauses as a pre-requisite for pressing ahead with any of *Programme for Action*. Wilson retorted that this would destroy the TUC's credibility. The union answer was in effect: "Either you do things your way or we do things our way. You can't have both."

The same argument bubbled to the surface at the next Downing Street conclave. The Prime Minister still insisted that there was a "missing link" (an image that, with "copper-bottomed compromise", became a *leitmotif* of the negotiations) in the TUC's proposals. What was required, Wilson said, was a balanced Bill matching rights and obligations. If the TUC could really produce some-thing effective, then the Government would consider dropping the penal clauses.

The union reply was sharp, and for once uncompromis-ing. The TUC was being asked to pay for "elementary trade union rights" by accepting penal clauses. "We are being asked to buy a package and we will not. The Government has talked of balance, but our judgment is that the price is too high. It is not possible to have a statutory and a voluntary policy running together. The two policies cannot and will not run side by side." The general council added that its proposals were more realistic than the Government's.

Barbara Castle again insisted that the TUC proposals were neither precise nor certain enough in their effects. The Government was looking for a demonstration of will. "In concrete terms, this means that action and penalties have to be taken against unconstitutional strikers, and that this action has to be clearly spelled out."

The TUC responded with a brief and wounded lecture. The general council could not accept the Government's idea that the answer had always to be a return to work in isolation from a settlement. The Government had complained that the TUC proposed to do nothing about unconstitutional stoppages, but as soon as they clarified the document to put beyond doubt what was intended the Government disparaged the solution and asked for more. "The Government appears not to be interested in a TUC alternative. The continued emphasis on getting people back to work, rather than on securing an agreed settlement of a dispute, underlines the fallacies in the Government's whole approach. The aim must be to prevent disputes and, if they arise, to settle them."

At this meeting, on 21 May, the Ministers did, however, repeat their undertaking not to introduce the Industrial Relations Bill until after the TUC's special congress at Croydon. In the interval, Harold Wilson and Barbara Castle had an uncomfortable Sunday evening at Chequers with Victor Feather, John Newton and the two most militant, most powerful members of the general council, Jack Jones and Hugh Scanlon. The initiative for this top-secret country-house dinner came from Feather. The Prime Minister seemed obsessed with the idea that Jones and Scanlon were the main obstacles to his proposals. Feather tried to convince him that this was not so. Yes, the new leaders of the Transport and General and the Amalgamated Engineers were fiercely critical, but opposition within the general council was much wider. (In fact not all of the union leaders had the same stomach for the fight.) Still, if Wilson needed persuading, why didn't he see Jones and Scanlon? At least, he would discover how intense their hostility was.

Feather undertook to bring them together, and agreed that Wilson could invite Barbara Castle. The question then was where could they meet without being spotted. Downing Street was dismissed as too public. The same objection was raised to a hotel suite, and the Prime Minister offered Chequers. A date was made for Sunday, 1 June.

Wilson describes the dinner-table discussion, which went on till after midnight, as "friendly but tough". The union participants accept this reading. They were, after all, the Prime Minister's guests at his country house. They were not going to sell any passes, but they recognised the mutual obligations of guests and host. And for all their proletarian truculence, they were just a touch impressed by the sixteenth-century mansion in its Chiltern hollow.

Jack Jones was allotted a top-floor bedroom known in the Chequers guide book as the "Prison Room". Lady Mary Grey, sister of Lady Jane Grey and great-granddaughter of Henry VII, had been imprisoned there for two years by order of Queen Elizabeth. She was considered a danger because she was an heir to the throne (Lady Jane had been Queen for nine days, but it had cost her her head). Lady Mary had also offended Elizabeth by marrying the Sergeant Porter to the Court without the Queen's consent. Facsimiles of some of the piteous letters she wrote to Sir William Cecil, later Lord Burleigh, imploring him to use his influence with the Queen to get her out, are kept in the room. There are also traces of a Latin inscription she wrote on the wall.

Jones evidently was not cowed. Nor did any of the

company draw contemporary lessons from the life mask of Oliver Cromwell, which Wilson took out of a drawer to show them. The nearest to acrimony was a private conversation between Wilson and Scanlon, when the engineers' president reminded the Prime Minister of Stalin's famous question: "How many divisions has the Pope?" The repartee soon advanced from Joseph Vissarionovich. Scanlon told Wilson the Labour movement did not want another Ramsay MacDonald. Wilson replied that he had no intention of being another Mac-Donald. Nor did he intend to be another Dubcek. "Get your tanks off my lawn, Hughie!"

Feather left on the Monday morning satisfied that the meeting had proved his point. Wilson and Castle knew now at first hand, without any public posturing, what the union attitudes were. Jones and Scanlon would not move another inch. Wilson was disturbed by a comment from Scanlon that any fines imposed on strikers would be met by sympathetic demonstrations, perhaps even by strikes and collections to pay the fines. "I knew the militants of Merseyside well enough," he writes in his own account, "to know that this would be extremely likely there, and no legislation—ours or the proposed Conservative legislation—could deal with it." None the less, the Prime Minister stood his ground. After the Croydon congress, he would still expect another move by the TUC, "involving a readiness by its constituent unions to discipline those responsible for unconstitutional action".

Instead of leaving it at that, Barbara Castle followed the Prime Minister's nudge with a three-page letter delivered by hand to Feather's office on the Tuesday evening, less than two days before the Croydon congress. The letter raised a new set of detailed points about the TUC's proposals and the Government's which Ministers would want to re-examine with the general council. Feather was annoyed and distressed. He and John Newton had worked hard to marshal a united general council behind the TUC programme. If the acting general secretary laid the letter before the general council when it gathered at 9.30 a.m. on 5 June, he knew he would be putting that unity at risk. Union leaders would have no time to grapple with the letter's implications, and when the congress opened at 10 a.m. it would do so amid needless confusion. Not only would hope of an acceptable deal with the Government evaporate, but some of the more bellicose unions might withdraw their consent from the *Programme for Action*. So, flexibility being the key, Feather pocketed the letter and said nothing before the congress.

Later in the day, when the general council met again before leaving Croydon, Feather quietly reported that he had received another letter from St James's Square. It was very complicated. His office would let them have copies to consider at leisure, then it could be dealt with in the normal way through committee. By then, the special congress, the first since the 1920s, had pledged its overwhelming support for the programme. The voting was 7,908,000 to 846,000. Not a single major union voted against the general council recommendations.

Feather was content. Congress had given him the kind of powers he had always sought for dealing with strikes and inter-union conflicts. He hoped, too, that the eight-one majority would convince the Government that the TUC would honour its bond. Who knows, Harold and Barbara might even drop him a note of appreciation. But no. The Department of Employment and Productivity issued a remote and critical press statement. Barbara

Castle still wanted her pound of flesh. Many members of the general council concluded that the Government did not want an agreement. If that was what Ministers preferred, that was what they must have. But let it be clear then that the choice was theirs and not the TUC's. Croydon was the end of the TUC's pliancy. The union leaders had talked or browbeaten their delegations into backing *Programme for Action*. The suspicions and defence of a lifetime had been abandoned. None of the general council would risk coaxing their members beyond Croydon. In any case the unions could make no further concessions of significance before the normal September congress, and Harold Wilson was still thinking in terms of a Bill in the current session.

On 9 June the general council trooped again into Downing Street for a ritual baring of fangs. The Government, Feather said, should not underestimate the TUC's achievement in winning such solid backing for its programme. Unions would not be so foolhardy as to ignore TUC advice against the whole weight of the trade union movement. Perhaps not, but "at the end of the day" the Government would have to be satisfied that the unions concerned had done all in their power to resolve the situation. The armies withdrew to their tents, agreeing to meet again two days later.

A string of meetings followed, spread over two evenings, 11 June and 12 June. Sometimes the Prime Minister and his Employment Secretary met the full general council, sometimes a negotiating subcommittee. Sometimes the general council met alone. The finance and general purposes committee, which would have been the logical bargaining agent, was bypassed because Jack Jones and Hugh Scanlon, as relative newcomers to the general council, were not yet members. Harold Wilson was still pushing for a change to Rule 11. If the Government was to drop penal sanctions, it would have to be satisfied about the effectiveness of the TUC's proposals, *"as well as their acceptability to public opinion"*. If the general council would legislate, the Prime Minister said, the Government would agree not to legislate. The Ministers went so far as to suggest a form of amendment to Rule 11, but the TUC was not biting.

The general council did, however, throw the Government a lifebelt. Its subcommittee had drafted a "clarification" of Rule 11 which would go to all unions as part of a general circular about the implication of the Croydon decisions. Feather had mentioned this possibility to the Prime Minister at one of their tête-à-têtes on 10 June. The general council labelled it unambiguously as "the limit of the possible compromise", but Wilson and Castle still believed they could reach the shore by their own efforts. The lifebelt was left floating, with an undertaking by the TUC that if a compromise could be reached the general council would co-operate with the Government in explaining the position to the country.

The climactic meeting between Ministers and unions was fixed for Wednesday, 18 June. Harold Wilson had promised to indicate to the general council "what the Government had in mind". Up to now, he and Barbara Castle had the general, if queasy, blessing of their colleagues; but the moment had come for a full reappraisal by the Cabinet, which met throughout the day on 17 June. Wilson acknowledges in his book that "many Ministers urged that we should drop all ideas of legislation and be content to accept the tremendous move forward which the imminence of legislation had forced the TUC to take".

But neither Wilson nor Castle was yet prepared to settle on such terms.

The Prime Minister might even have carried the day but for an unsignalled intervention by his Chief Whip, Bob Mellish. The Chief Whip is not a member of the Cabinet, but attends its meetings as an officer of the party. Usually he does not speak unless spoken to, but Mellish is not the kind to hide his light under protocol. He had spoken before in Cabinet, and he was going to speak again. His message was simple and devastating: "It's not on. You're not going to get this legislation through the Commons. You're wasting your time."

Mellish was the nearest the Labour Party of the sixties had to a Tammany Hall "boss" south of the Tees. He had been a Transport and General Workers' official in the London docks (the youngest ever appointed by Ernest Bevin). During the war he rose from private to major because, on his own testimony, he was the only man in the regiment who could read a manifest. As heir to Herbert Morrison, Mellish ruled the London Labour Party with a strong right hand. Ever since his appointment as Chief Whip on 30 April, he had been making his assessment of backbench opinion on Barbara Castle's Bill. Mellish himself was sponsored by the Transport and General Workers. What he called "the men on the middle ground", his own unrebellious trade union core of the Parliamentary Labour Party, were found to be united almost to a man against the proposals. If you took the dissenters of the *Tribune* Left and the unsponsored trade unionists and added them to the trade union group, more than half the parliamentary party was against the Bill.

Mellish's interjection did not turn the Cabinet tide. The first waves were already breaking on the beach. What

Mellish provided was the force eight gale to speed them up the sea wall. As Wilson concedes, "Hawk-eyed opponents of the Bill were probably right in their calculations that, by lunch-time, a majority of the Cabinet had expressed either their opposition to the Bill, or at least strong reservations about it." Even Roy Jenkins had defected—not because he was against the legislation in principle, but because by June he felt that it was too late. Besides, Ministers had created too great an expectation of a negotiated settlement with the TUC for them to force a Bill through. The Chancellor was ready to compromise, though with no great sense of triumph. That evening, after the Cabinet had broken, Mellish accompanied Wilson to a meeting with the trade union group of MPs. From the Chief Whip's corner of the committee room, the hostility there confirmed all that he had said in Cabinet.

On the evidence of his own published account, Wilson was still not convinced that his policy was in ashes. A number of Cabinet Ministers indicated privately that if it came to a crisis they would back him. When Wilson met Feather that night he told the acting general secretary that he "held the proxies", and warned him against messages that he could not carry the Cabinet. Feather was tempted to laugh in the Prime Minister's face. He had talked again to Douglas Houghton and knew the position in the Parliamentary Labour Party. Regardless of the Cabinet, Feather could feel the trout on the end of his line.

Barbara Castle had fewer illusions than her leader. The Employment Secretary went to bed on 17 June prepared to resign if she and Wilson could not extract a presentable formula from the TUC. She believed that the Prime Minister was just as ready to go. In more liberated moments, she even relished the prospect of returning to the

Cabinet room and saying: "Hard luck. We couldn't get anything. Your move."

Other members of the Wilson Cabinet are still satisfied that if he had come back without a compromise and tried to brazen it out, the Prime Minister would have been defeated. He did not hold *enough* proxies, though there is independent evidence of some. What would have happened then can only be conjectured, but not all of those Ministers opposing the Industrial Relations Bill wanted a change of leader. There were some—younger Ministers like Peter Shore and Judith Hart among them—who owed their advancement to Wilson and still regarded him as the best Prime Minister they had.

When Wilson opened the doors of No. 10 to the general council for the eighth and final time on the morning of 18 June, he and Barbara Castle had only one card left to play: "You can wreck us, but we can wreck you too. Put us out and you put the Tories in, with a mandate to cut the unions down to size." The point was taken, as it had been all along, though with more realism perhaps than grace. The Prime Minister began by again demanding a change of rule. The general council again replied that Rule 11 as it appeared in *Programme for Action* was sufficient. Hugh Scanlon added that he could not be sure of steering further changes through the engineers' national committee, his fifty-two member policy-making body, which would have to be recalled. It had been hard enough for Croydon. Support would be even more precarious for the September congress at Portsmouth. The significance of this argument was recognised both by the Ministers and the general council. The engineering union was the second biggest in the TUC, and the engineering industry had more unofficial strikes than any other. A change of rule would have been worthless if it had been repudiated by the engineers.

It was time to bring out the old lifebelt. Fred Hayday, number two in the hierarchy of the General and Municipal Workers' Union but an elder of the TUC, impressed on the Prime Minister how "solemn and binding" their undertaking would be. The general council would adapt the Government's wording for its "clarification" of Rule 11, Croydon style, and guarantee to carry it out. Jack Jones reinforced Hayday's case by drawing a comparison with the Bridlington Principles. The 1939 congress at Bridlington had established a code of behaviour governing inter-union competition for members. The declaration was not a rule, but it had the same authority. The amplified Rule 11 would be just as binding.

Hayday's union had been the most consistently loyal to the Labour Government since 1964, Jones's had been the most critical. Yet between them—and with the eager endorsement of their colleagues—they had assembled a face-saver. During the lunch break Wilson and Barbara Castle, with legal window-dressing supplied by the Attorney-General, Elwyn Jones, drafted the Downing Street Declaration. With the general council's blessing, Feather again met Wilson and Castle. He emphasised that there could be no change of rule; that a declaration would be more binding and more effective; and that such an undertaking would be unanimous. The Prime Minister was still playing hard to get, but Feather was confident the battle was over. He could read the tea-leaves as well as anyone. Bluffs were exchanged for the last time when the full meeting resumed. The union leaders were cross rather than depressed. Wilson was still haggling over the details. But eventually the ministerial draft was accepted with only

In at the deep end: inaugurating union swimming pool, Brighton 1970

In Ripon Street,
1971, during a snow
storm

minor amendment. The compact was endorsed by the waiting Cabinet. The penal clauses were dead. Long live the Downing Street Declaration.

The final round had lasted longer than either side had hoped. The Cabinet had originally been called for noon, but was stood down till 5.15 p.m., A noble pillar of the TUC general council approached Victor Feather at the beginning of the morning session and asked if he could get away by lunchtime. The answer was blunt and Bradford, but why the hurry? Well, the man said, he had managed to land a couple of fifty shilling tickets for Royal Ascot and he didn't want to disappoint his lady. Alas, she had to wait another year. But Ascot was not entirely neglected. Feather and two other members of the general council had picked up a tip. They borrowed a Downing Street telephone during one of the breaks and rang a bookmaker. To complete the acting general secretary's day, his horse, Lucyrowe, won the Coronation Stakes at 15 to 8.

The last argument between Wilson and the TUC was over the "unanimity" of the declaration. The Prime Minister wanted all thirty-nine elected members of the general council to sign the "solemn and binding" document. Feather, who was taking neither chances nor dictation, insisted that the declaration be signed by himself and John Newton on behalf of them all. As he put his pen away, Wilson was heard to mutter: "There'll be some blood flowing after this." According to the TUC minutes, the Prime Minister "expressed the hope that the outcome of the discussions would be regarded as a victory for good industrial relations, a view which was fully endorsed by the general council".

Amen, but was it a defeat for Harold Wilson and

L

Barbara Castle? If, as his book implies, Wilson thinks it was anything less, he is alone in that belief among the three senior Ministers most committed in advance to the legislation. He had demanded a TUC law in return for a law of the land. The TUC had not given it to him. The TUC had offered a week earlier to circularise a "binding statement of intent". The unions may have moved "farther in a month than in forty years", but they had not moved anything like as far as Wilson and Castle had demanded. In particular, there would still be no automatic return to work while a settlement was being negotiated in unofficial strikes. Feather would have more power of intervention than any previous general secretary, but he would still have to "do the best we can".

It is an old principle of the Labour clubs where Victor Feather was reared that a card-player on a winning streak never skins his opponent down to his last penny. You leave him a scrap of dignity and his bus fare home. That was what Feather believed he was doing when he gave his solemn and binding undertaking. Nevertheless, his respect for Wilson and Barbara Castle—as Labour leaders and as bargainers—had diminished. They had chained themselves to a foolish policy and had defended it with neither flexibility nor resilience.

Feather is not a man for vendettas, but he has an unforgiving memory. A month after the Downing Street concordat, Judith Hart, one of the Ministers known to have fought the Bill in Cabinet, was one of the two principal speakers at the Durham Miners' Gala. She arrived a few minutes late for the annual dinner the evening before, and as she took her seat at the top table Feather rose half-way down the hall. Although they hardly knew each other, he went to greet her with a warm and public handshake. Harold and Mary Wilson sat silently at an adjoining table.

Feather's bitterness towards Barbara Castle cut deeper. He felt—justly or otherwise—that the Employment Secretary had tried to run with the hares of the Left and hunt with the hounds of the Right. Feather's memories of her family were as affectionate as ever, though he and Barbara were not exact contemporaries and had not been particularly close in their Bradford years. He would still trust her on any personal question, banter reminiscences with her on Yorkshire Television, and even speak on her election platform. But after 1969, he would be very careful about taking her at her word on political matters.

CHAPTER THIRTEEN

Mr General Secretary

LIKE THE secretary-general of the United Nations, the general secretary of the Trades Union Congress is a man of much influence and little power. An individual union derives its strength from the number of its members; its dominant or strategic position in an industry or craft; and the readiness of the rank and file to follow their leaders. The National Union of Mineworkers could hobble the economy in a month. A fistful of maintenance electricians could deprive the nation of its newspapers overnight. Ernest Bevin, leader of the Transport and General Workers' Union, could demolish George Lansbury, leader of the Labour Party. But the TUC, in spite of its affiliated membership of ten million workers, can do no more than its constituent unions will permit. The limits, however, are flexible. They can be stretched by the aspiration and guile of the general secretary; the range and quality of the service Congress House offers the unions; and the authority with which it presents a trade union perspective to Governments.

Every general secretary, from Walter Citrine to Victor Feather, has striven in his own style to extend and deepen the TUC's influence. Citrine, the creator of the modern TUC, defined the targets and the tactics for them all. His early reasoning, he recalls in *Men and Work*, was that he "must try to make the TUC indispensable to the affiliated unions; to establish a leadership which they would be willing to follow; to demonstrate the capacity of the general council really to act as the general staff that most progressive trade unionists wanted". The trade union movement had to exert its influence in an ever-widening sphere and not be contained within its traditional walls. "We must try to expand the activities of the TUC until we could establish an efficient system whereby the TUC would be regularly and naturally consulted by whatever Government was in power on any subject of direct concern to the unions."

Forty years later, George Woodcock echoed his old chief with his ambition to lead the TUC "out of Trafalgar Square and into Whitehall". The trade unions, he argued in a *Guardian* interview on 29 April 1966, shared a responsibility for working people with Governments. They had to seek means of working with Governments in this mutual responsibility. "This is the heart of everything to me. All the rest is detail. It comes down to the basis on which we can genuinely co-operate."

The techniques, too, have hardly varied down the years. Citrine was a great organiser. He recruited carefully and perceptively, balancing university graduates with men like Feather who had the Labour movement in their bones. The aim was to create a secretariat that was much more efficient and resourceful than anything an individual union could match. Then the unions, however jealous of their autonomy, would have to approach the TUC to act on their behalf in matters outside their own industries.

The task has never been easy. Low's carthorse is a surly beast, ill-designed for changes of pace or direction. To proclaim your ideas from the housetops, Citrine concluded, would only invite opposition. The thing to do was to "act on the assumption that these were already features of the accepted policy of the TUC and to prosecute them steadfastly but not noisily". Citrine applied this principle of reform by stealth to everything from hiring his first economist to introducing the genteel rostrum to the 1928 congress.

Soon after Citrine's election as general secretary in 1926, Arthur Henderson, his long-serving Labour counterpart, proffered a little avuncular advice: "Never fight your council. Always wait until you have heard their opinions before you give your own." TUC general secretaries have tended to alternate between those like Citrine and Woodcock who prodded and provoked from the front, and those like Tewson and Feather who chose their time in the middle of a general council debate. All, however, have recognised the underlying sense of Henderson's lesson. If you fight the council, you will lose. Woodcock pinned it with a metaphor. He "played for a draw". A paper majority, he always said, was useless if the minority included some of the biggest unions. There had to be a consensus, though he emphasised his independence by introducing his congress speeches with: "Woodcock, TUC".

Feather's three predecessors all left their marks. Citrine gave the TUC the stamp of his own self-reliance. Between 1939 and 1945 the TUC's part in mobilising industry for the war completed a phase of involvement that began with Ernest Bevin's membership of the Macmillan Committee on the finance and credit system and with the Mond–Turner conferences of 1928–29 that took the TUC into the board room. Vincent Tewson's monument is Congress House, a building and a symbol, opened in March 1958. Woodcock's pride is that the TUC accepted

its seats on the National Economic Development Council
in 1962, though many union leaders had wanted to boycott that principal meeting ground of Government,
business and labour. Woodcock felt he had persuaded a
peacetime TUC to transform itself from a permanent
opposition to a partner in the economic process.

Victor Feather had to wait a working lifetime for his
chance to join them in the TUC pantheon. At the end of
the afternoon session on Tuesday, 2 September 1969,
more than thirty-two years after he had left Bradford to
work as an assistant in the organisation department for £5
a week, the Portsmouth congress elected him unopposed
as general secretary. There was no fanfare of trumpets, no
roll of drums. Congress had finished its discussion of
Raynaud's Phenomenon, a palsy common among men
who work with pneumatic drills or power saws. The chairman of the scrutineers, Mr D. Currie of the Clerical and
Administrative Workers, was called to announce the
result of that year's multiple ballot. He read solemnly
through the twenty trade groups of the general council
and the "general purposes committee" (the one that looks
after conference arrangements). Then came, "General
secretary (no contest): Feather, Victor—elected", followed
almost immediately by the names of the lucky pair elected
to bear the TUC's fraternal greetings to the Canadian
trade unions. A delegate formally seconded the adoption
of the report. The report was adopted. Congress adjourned
for the day. The official minutes stopped referring to him
as "acting general secretary".

Feather made his first speech as general secretary in the
industrial relations debate the next morning. With an
implicit sense of occasion, he restated the fundamentals:
"The TUC never has been and never will be some-

thing separate and apart from the unions, sitting in judgment on them. I never talk of TUC authority or union discipline, or a chain of command. Unions are independent voluntary organisations and the TUC is their federal body. We move by discussion, persuasion and agreement.

"A man's union is what enables him to stand up for his rights as a worker. It is his guarantee that others—his workmates, his employer, the Government itself—will respect his dignity. The TUC is here to express and defend the rights that are common to all trade unionists. But the interests of employees can on occasion come into conflict with each other. That, too, is what the TUC is here for—to try to reconcile, as far as is humanly possible, conflicts of interest that inevitably emerge between different groups of organised workers from time to time. Unions agreed a long time ago that the general body of organised labour—the TUC and its general council—should be entitled to express a view, should have the right to comment on a general situation, and to advise on a particular problem—even the right to criticise when the actions of one union have an unfair effect on others in our movement. . . .

"We are under growing pressure to justify our actions. We all live and work in a world that is changing and we have to be ready to modify our methods, while preserving the essential purposes of trade unionism. But there would be a lot less trouble in industry if managements were more ready to alter their attitudes, too.

"Trade unionists are sometimes accused of being slow to change. Well, it is not a serious defect to be cautious. It is often a basic job of unions to question a change and to insist that those who want it should demonstrate that it is desirable. It is always a basic job of unions to insist that when there are changes, workpeople must share in the benefits."

After a passing reference to "the diversions of the last few months", the new general secretary returned to an old and favoured project. He attached "a very high priority" to arranging discussions with selected groupings of unions, probably on an industry basis, to see how they could co-operate in improving their service to the workers and improving industrial relations. The first six of these conferences, covering all the affiliated unions, had been held in March to ponder the implications of the Donovan Report. Feather suggested now that they should be guided by four requirements:

"While we continue to accept our share of responsibility for the efficient conduct of the industries where our members work, and our obligations to society as a whole, we must do so as independent organisations which make decisions of our own. We must as unions and the TUC be more strongly representative. This means more recruitment; but also clearer spheres of influence and better communications. We must devise a new strategy for serving our members and promoting their interests. We have also got to ensure that our administration is efficient. The best thought-out policies are of little use unless the nuts and bolts are there."

It was a deliberately reassuring speech, delivered in a minor, almost conversational key. The nearest to a Feather joke was the suggestion that come the revolution they would name a street "June 18 Street" (in a later, more flippant speech he nailed the redesignation to Downing Street). The challenge was there, but it was muted. Feather was stressing first principles for the benefit of

Harold Wilson and Barbara Castle, as well as for their Conservative opponents. He was also drawing a line at the end of the Woodcock chapter. The Feather TUC would be less concerned with the corridors of Whitehall than with the factory and the branch room. The new general secretary wanted to bring the unions into Congress House. He was not spurning philosophy, but he saw it more as a philosophy of the trade union movement than as a philosophy of government. And he wanted that philosophy explained in the places where people could carry it into effect. Whitehall and Trafalgar Square are not mutually exclusive. Nelson stands in one and looks down the other. But even at this stage, with a Labour Government still in office, Feather was choosing to change the balance.

As Fleet Street was quick to point out, Feather was a "man in a hurry". He was sixty-one, the oldest by far of the five general secretaries appointed in the previous half century. It is an almost sacred trade union precept that officials retire at sixty-five, often on their sixty-fifth birthday. The TUC has no rule to that effect, but it was very unlikely that the general council would allow Feather to continue for more than a few months after April 1973. The Feather era was restricted to four years. It is possible that he deliberately, therefore, limited his ambitions to the familiar and the attainable. Possible but not probable. The ideas he expounded in his first speech, and the direction in which he tried to propel the TUC, were not the product of a few hectic months. They grew out of the experience and frustrations of his nine years as assistant general secretary. Feather is a man of well-tended roots. He had spent his life in "organisation". He wanted to recast the TUC in his own image.

CHAPTER FOURTEEN

A gallon in a pint pot

IN THE CONVALESCENT year between 18 June 1969, and 18 June 1970, when the Conservatives returned to office under Edward Heath, Victor Feather worked ostentatiously both to reconcile the political and industrial wings of Labour and to honour the solemn and binding compact he had signed that Wednesday afternoon in Downing Street. Harold Wilson was invited to address the Portsmouth congress, the second time he had done so as Prime Minister. His message, delivered and received without apparent irony, was: "It is a mark of the maturity, the influence of the trade union movement in our democracy that no Government could proceed very far with the development of its economic policy except on the basis of consultation with the organised trade union movement. It is still more a mark of the common purpose of the Labour movement as a whole that no Labour Government would want to." In an even more explicit effort to cover the scar tissues, John Newton purred in his presidential address: "The trade union movement acclaims no victories. Victories are for boys who play at games. The movement measures its achievements by the improvements it secures for the workpeople it represents. Whatever success was achieved in June this year it should now be seen as the success of the British Labour movement."

The TUC began to collect and publish statistics of disputes in which it had intervened. The general council proudly informed the Brighton congress in September 1970, that more than 180 disputes had been reported to Congress House in the twelve months ending in June 1970. This was contrasted with a figure of only forty reported in the twelve months before the special congress at Croydon.

"Most disputes were reported by affiliated organisations in accordance with the new Rules 11 and 12, but some were brought to the TUC by the Department of Employment and Productivity when their conciliation officers were unable to find an acceptable solution and some by employers who sought the assistance of the TUC direct. In about two-thirds of the cases reported there was an actual or threatened stoppage of work. Nearly half the cases reported concerned inter-union problems, of which sixty-three related to membership and the application of the Bridlington Principles and twenty-four were demarcation or other problems reported under Rule 12.

"The number of unions concerned directly or indirectly in the 180 disputes was forty-five, some unions being involved in a number of cases. Nearly 1,000 contacts were made with these unions by telephone, through correspondence or at meetings. In nearly fifty cases the TUC general secretary personally met the unions involved, sometimes on more than one occasion, and on about twenty occasions he also met representatives of the management, including representatives of employers' associations.

"The disputes in which the TUC gave assistance in finding a formula which led to a more speedy conclusion varied in size from ten workers (whose strike caused some

2,500 other workers to be laid off) to over 120,000 workers who had already lost nearly one million working days. In some disputes workers were taking selective action (e.g. one-day strikes) and TUC assistance helped to contain such disputes to the minimum. In about thirty cases, TUC intervention helped to avert altogether a stoppage of work which was already threatened or which could have developed if a solution to the particular problem had not been found."

Like the astute public relations presentation that it was, the TUC report hesitated to make extravagant claims about how much it had saved industry in working days or union members in pay packets. Its "rough guess" was that the figure of days saved lay between two and a half and three million between June 1969, and June 1970. On this basis, the amount of pay saved "must have been" well over £10 million.

"It is also difficult to say with certainty on whose initiative some of the disputes were eventually resolved. However, disputes on which the assistance of the TUC is sought are likely to be the most intractable. On no occasion has any union refused the TUC's invitation to discuss a particular dispute."

Undoubtedly, the TUC did its manful best. So did its new general secretary with his fifty eager interventions. But the general council report tells only part of the story. Between January and July 1970, the number of days lost through strikes was almost double that for January–July 1969. At 6,054,000 it was higher than for any year since the 1930s. The main reason for the increase was the gradual relaxation of incomes restraint in the run-up to the general election. The dam had burst, the wage claims flowed through. The unions had three years' fettered bargaining to make good and were ready for a fight. Inevitably the Conservatives blamed the increase on the Downing Street surrender. The experience of their own first three years suggests, however, that a tough approach makes little difference if the workers are angry, determined, or avaricious enough to force their demands on reluctant employers.

The Downing Street agreement of June 1969, was not a panacea. Its limits were those of the TUC's relationship to its constituent unions and of the tribal world of industrial relations itself. No one believed otherwise. What it did achieve, though, was to stretch the scope of TUC intervention, and to remove any residual distrust—particularly on the old Left of the general council—of Vic Feather, Hammer of the Comms. By keeping the argument with Harold Wilson firmly on the ground, Feather had strengthened his bonds with union leaders. The most valuable, if least spectacular, advance was the new power to intervene in inter-union conflicts. But the big public disputes into which Feather was drawn in his first year as general secretary tended to demonstrate how little had actually been changed by the solemn and binding declaration. Industrial crises were still messy. Strikes were sometimes justified. Peacemaking remained as uncertain as it was unscientific.

The first test of TUC intervention in an unofficial dispute came barely a month after Downing Street. The general council set out to show that the new powers would not be used automatically to slap down unofficial strikers if they had a genuine grievance. It ordered 1,300 blast-furnacemen back to work at the British Steel Corporation's Margam plant in Port Talbot, but insisted that wage negotiations must be started immediately. Unless a satisfactory solution was reached within a week of their return, the men's union should declare the strike official. The TUC also noted the "long-standing" nature of the labour problems at Margam and asked Barbara Castle to set up an inquiry.

The blastfurnacemen, who contended that they had been unreasonably excluded from a national wage agreement, refused to go back to work. Another 10,000 men were laid off in consequence. Feather went to South Wales for "secret" talks with the strikers, but failed then and on a second visit to persuade them to return. The trouble at Port Talbot was a result of inadequate management, saddled with a clumsy attempt by the Steel Corporation to impose ill-considered change, and of a weak and disintegrating union. Barbara Castle appointed a court of inquiry under Professor Donald Robertson, which eventually awarded the strikers the £1 a week they had demanded.

The stoppage lasted eight weeks and was vindicated by the court of inquiry. The TUC immediately offered to help the men's union, the National Union of Blastfurnacemen, to reorganise itself. Congress House also made available the services of a TUC productivity adviser. It was the first time the TUC had involved itself in the internal affairs of a union simply because it was falling down on the job.

"Long before the TUC leaders made their solemn and binding declaration to the Prime Minister," John Torode wrote in the *Guardian* on 22 August 1969, "Mr Feather was stressing that the purpose of the exercise was not to clobber every worker who stepped outside procedure. As the Donovan Commission pointed out, procedures are often inadequate and outdated.

"Building on this argument, the TUC stressed that employers as well as men often exploited or ignored procedure and so provoked strikes which were technically unconstitutional. The TUC insisted that it would only order men back to work where the employers were beyond reproach. But the union chiefs did not consider the situation in which men were in effect striking against their own inadequate union structure as well as shifty bosses . . . Port Talbot has guaranteed that they must in future. . . .

"Mr Wilson wanted automatic penalties against unconstitutional strikers. Rightly, the union bosses refused. They wanted flexibility to deal with each case on its merits. They offered to deal with the root causes of bad industrial relations at a plant, not the symptom. Now they must prove they mean business by building a better union for blastfurnacemen."

In fact the TUC did nothing of the sort. The general secretary's inventive mind moved on to the next forty-nine disputes awaiting his intervention that year. With no pressure from Congress House, there was a change at the top in the steel men's union. The new leader was left to get on with it.

The durability of the old ways was demonstrated no less painfully in a ten-week strike by 1,150 workers at the Standard-Triumph car plant on Merseyside. The strikers walked out in support of a pay claim in total disregard of negotiating procedure. Their action was unofficial, but threatened much of the motor industry. Barbara Castle again had to fall back on a court of inquiry, the time-honoured way of negotiating out of a corner under the cloak of judicial impartiality. The men won their ninepence an hour.

The other limitation on TUC peacemaking—the jealously-preserved autonomy of individual unions—was illustrated in the spring of 1970 by the unofficial strike of 11,000 workers in Pilkingtons' glass factories, mainly in St Helens. The stoppage began over money, but by the unhappy end of its seven weeks it had become a campaign against managerial paternalism and union complacency. Again, thousands of jobs outside the glassworks were threatened, mainly in the motor industry which is geared to a steady flow of components, often from firms outside its own control.

Victor Feather tried to make peace between the rank and file strike committee at St Helens and the national leadership of their union, the General and Municipal Workers, the third biggest in the TUC. The GMWU is traditionally strong in Lancashire, but it is not celebrated, there or nationally, for the militancy of its full-time officials. The Pilkington men felt neglected and under-consulted. Feather chanced his arm by inviting the rebellious strike leaders to London, but carefully spelled out his conditions. The talks could not begin until there had been a return to work. He dangled the possibility, but no more, of agreements on victimisation and reinstatement.

Feather was anxious to placate the strike leaders without alienating the GMWU. A settlement needed the co-operation and good will of both. The TUC general secretary had six telephone conversations with the chairman and vice-chairman of the strike committee. At their request he confirmed his invitation by telegram. "Confirming our phone conversation today," it read, "I give you an undertaking that, following a resumption of work, arrangements will be put in hand immediately for you and

M

the strike committee representatives to meet here—at the TUC headquarters—to thrash out all difficulties and differences that have arisen, with a view to ensuring that this kind of situation will not occur again."

The TUC magic worked. The strikers went back and their leaders took the train to Euston. This first meeting between the strike committee and GMWU officials lasted seven hours. Members of the strike committee, quoted by Tony Lane and Kenneth Roberts of Liverpool University in their *Strike at Pilkingtons*, reported that Feather had been an admirable and impartial chairman. The talks, however, were inconclusive. The GMWU made no concessions, and the strike leaders decided to go home with nothing more tangible than Feather's offer of continued mediation.

A week later the strike committee asked Feather to arrange another meeting with their union leaders. The GMWU agreed, provided the strike committee stopped attacking the union. The strike leaders concurred and returned to London. This second meeting, planned for 2 June, never took place. A TUC spokesman told the waiting press that fifteen minutes before Feather was due to welcome the two sides, Lord Cooper, the GMWU general secretary, had telephoned to say that the union team would not be coming. "Loyal" Pilkington shop stewards were refusing to meet the rebels, who were said to be continuing their campaign against the union. Cooper added, according to the *Daily Telegraph*, that since the strike was over the unofficial strike committee should disband.

Feather was angry at the way he had been treated by Cooper. The strike leaders, who had already suffered a fortnight of humiliation, felt betrayed. But there was nothing more Feather could do. The scruples of the loyal shop stewards remain the official explanation of Cooper's refusal to go to Congress House. But like that of the wolves who ate the rabbits in the Thurber fable, his message was clear: it was now a purely internal matter. Cooper had asserted his authority within his own union. It was, perhaps, a little late in the day, but since the strike was over and no other jobs were at risk, Feather had exhausted his possibilities.

The general secretaryship, at a yearly salary of about £5,500 (paid weekly in cash), made little difference to Victor Feather's style of life. Instead of pouring a quart into his pint pot, he tried now to condense a gallon. He was still one of the first to arrive at Congress House, often reaching his fourth-floor office, overlooking Jacob Epstein's tough-tender war memorial to the trade union dead, by 8.30 a.m., and one of the last to leave. He kept one efficient secretary, who had worked with or for him since 1941, but recruited no personal assistant. He had a chauffeur to drive him around London, but usually travelled alone and by train (first class) outside the capital.

In March 1970, Feather was elected a member of Grillions, Britain's oldest political dining club founded in 1812, which gathers fortnightly in Grosvenor House during the parliamentary session. Membership is limited to eighty-five. Between the middle of Queen Victoria's reign and the First World War, every British Prime Minister, Lord Chancellor and Foreign Secretary was a member. Gladstone attended its dinners for more than half a century. The 7th Earl of Derby praised its "generous and courteous comprehension of diversities of political views". Part of the Grillions appeal is that members can attend without giving notice. Gladstone once found himself there alone and consoled himself by drinking a whole bottle of champagne. Feather was the first TUC general secretary to be elected. Hugh Gaitskell was elected in 1952, and Labour members of the 1970s include James Callaghan and Roy Jenkins.

Feather was just as likely, however, to spend his Wednesday nights with the Luton Trades Council. Even as general secretary, he was reluctant to delegate the sort of fraternal hand-clasping he had relished all his TUC life. He was still the lad from Bradford, the lad from head office. He still needed the affection of his "community". If one of his colleagues offered to stand in for him, Feather would say: "Thank you, but old Fred has been telling his friends for six months that Vic Feather was coming to give him his silver badge. I can't let him down now."

With his new and welcomed access to television and radio, Feather the entertainer soon became a national figure. The wit may sometimes have been a little sub-Oscar Wilde ("What's the use of a hot line to Downing Street if all you get is the cold shoulder?"), but the general secretary of the TUC was a card. Like most politicians and union leaders, Feather was paid the going rate for feature and magazine programmes but not for news interviews. He remained enough, however, of an old-school comic to need the response and intimacy of a club audience. It kept him down to earth, and it saved him having to write new scripts for every performance.

The funniest speech in his first couple of years as general secretary was originally delivered to the 1970 congress at Brighton. The timing and pointing were exquisite. His manner was relaxed, the language familiar. And, as always, the message came through.

"Perhaps we are too modest, perhaps we are too self-effacing. The failures in relationships, of course, hit the headlines, but there is a great story to be told about industrial relations achievements. Dog bites man is not news. Man bites dog is news. That applies to industrial relations in particular. Certainly this year's strike record is worse than last year's, but before we get the hair shirts out let's have a look at that. What are the facts? Six million days were lost because of strikes in the first seven months of this year. That sounds a lot. But how many days could have been worked in those seven months? I make it 3,000 million. So we got 2,994 million and we lost only six million.

"A great number of people translate every wage application into percentages these days—$33\frac{1}{3}$, $37\frac{1}{2}$, 300 —you name it, they'll invent it. I know it is early in the morning, but perhaps you and I could do some fast mental arithmetic. 3,000 million—that is the one that is worked —6 million lost, so we lose 3,000 million divided by 6 million. Cross off the six noughts at the end—you can do it in your head! Six into 3,000 gives you 500. So the strike days are one to 500, a fifth of one per cent: we lost 0·2 of one per cent. We got 99·8 per cent—and it's worse than last year! A very bad deterioration—last year we got 99·9 per cent. We did not do so well in motor cars as we did in the others. There we got just over 99 per cent. That's a failure!

"Some of you have children. You have youngsters and they will be coming home. If one of them comes home and says, 'Dad'—or 'Joe' because they are more likely to call you 'Joe' these days—'In my GCE subjects I got 99·8 per cent in every subject', don't clout the kid! You've got a genius—he takes after his dad! You would be a sour parent if you looked at him and thought he was a potential juvenile delinquent and had pinched the examination papers out of the teacher's desk before the examination started. Be proud of the lad, else he might clout you!"

The argument went down better among the union professionals who dominate the dark-suited annual congress than it did at the Department of Employment and Productivity, or perhaps in the industrial relations units of the flourishing new business schools. But as the Yorkshire Television cameras following Feather from trades hall to trades hall through the length and breadth of provincial England unkindly revealed, Joe and his precocious offspring were good for a laugh for months afterwards.

A typical week's diary of Victor Feather, general secretary, read something like this:

Monday: 9 a.m.–10.30, Canadian students; 10.30–12.30, conference of departmental heads; 2 p.m., meeting with Sir Frank Figgures, director-general of the National Economic Development Council; 3, Social insurance department interview; 3.30, International department interview; 4, Dr Ellis (Barnardos); 5, Polish Ambassador; 6.15, speech on "Communications" to the London branch of the Chartered Institute of Secretaries.

Tuesday: In Birmingham all day for the TUC's Midland regional advisory council; return to London for dinner (Royal Society).

Wednesday: 10.30 a.m., NEDC (including lunch); 4 p.m., Port Talbot disputes committee; 5, meeting with

Prime Minister on unemployment; 5.30, Israeli reception; 6.30, British Airline Pilots' Association reception; 7.30, GLC staff association reception; Grillions. (How many of the receptions he reached is not recorded.)

Thursday: 7.55 a.m., King's Cross arriving Leeds 10.34; 2 p.m., opening of new offices in Bradford of the Dyers' and Bleachers' Union; 3.30, Leeds station arriving King's Cross 6.39; 7, meeting with Japanese union official.

Friday: 9 a.m., Swedish broadcasting; 9.30, Mr Spinelli (EEC); 10.30, press conference ("Good industrial relations"); 12, preliminary meeting with John Davies on restrictive practices legislation; 1.45 p.m., Paddington for Bristol (Harlech Television).

Saturday: 11.30 a.m., depart for Nassau, Bahamas, for meeting of American Federation of Labor–Congress of Industrial Organisations.

As general secretary, as in his more junior TUC days, Feather took no holidays (his wife usually had hers while Victor was away and busy at the annual congress). He seldom managed a whole day free from engagements, and an entire weekend in Northamptonshire was a rare luxury.

CHAPTER FIFTEEN

Dialogue of the deaf

"VIC'S TRAGEDY," one of his adversaries in the Battle of Downing Street was in the habit of saying, "was that he peaked on a negative." More tragically, Feather was stuck with a negative for most of the time after the Conservatives took office in June 1970. It was a period of Pyrrhic defeats and surly resistance for the trade unions; a period of dissension and suspensions in the TUC. Power receded not only from Congress House to the unions, but from the union leaders to their members. At times it looked as if Feather regarded demonstrations as an alternative to the policy-making and coordination that is the TUC's best rôle, but as general secretary he never quite severed his lines to Whitehall. Nor did he hand in his pass to the back door of Downing Street.

Within Congress House, Feather persevered with the creation and strengthening of industrial committees. The idea of providing a unified strategy and unified services for the multiplicity of unions in a particular industry was not new. George Woodcock had been dubious about it, but had eventually given it his blessing in principle. The steel committee, which was established to negotiate with the renationalised British Steel Corporation, was a first, frail flowering. Feather, who cherished the committees as a means of bringing the TUC into the places where it mattered, pressed the idea so hard that for the first two years of his regime his staff could hardly keep up. Progress inevitably was slow. The committees and their advocates had to overcome the suspicion of individual unions worried about their sovereignty. The older, more cumbersome federations—like those in engineering and printing —still had their champions and their vested interests. As compensation, however, Feather had the enthusiastic support of Jack Jones, whose Transport and General Workers' Union had grown by now to more than 1,500,000 members. Jones claimed that the industrial committees had first been mooted by his union, though paternity was disputed by Congress House officials.

The first committees formed or developed under Feather were in the construction trades, transport, local government and the health services. The pace and services varied from committee to committee. In steel, the TUC was drawn into negotiations—not on wages, but on pensions, sick pay, disputes procedures and the delimiting of inter-union spheres of influence. In local government, the TUC was involved in negotiating such matters as staff reorganisation and pensions. Again, it did not co-ordinate wage claims, but it did facilitate an exchange of information on different unions' demands. Each union could see what was going on around it and plan accordingly. The TUC secretariat soon proved its usefulness. It could put up ideas without grinding axes. It offered continuity, research, flexibility and the experience of other committees and other industries. The industrial committees attracted no spotlights, but if they proved to be Feather's principal bequest to the trade union movement he would not feel disappointed. The TUC would be taking one big, functional step nearer Citrine's vision of a trade union general staff.

Internationally, Feather's most pressing problem as general secretary was Britain's entry into the European

Economic Community, negotiated by the Conservative Government in the year between June 1970, and June 1971, and consummated with accession to the Treaty of Rome on 1 January 1973. Feather himself was broadly pro-Market, but the TUC like the rest of the Labour movement was swinging strongly "against the Tory terms". Feather could not fight his general council on the basic issue, but he managed to deflect it from demanding British withdrawal and to guide it into a wider "European" policy.

The unity of the European trade unions had been troubling the TUC ever since the creation of the Community of the Six. None of the attempts to link the unions of the Common Market countries and of the European Free Trade Association had succeeded. Feather inherited a strong office policy, drafted in the international department, in favour of a confederation embracing the unions of the enlarged Common Market and those of democratic Europe outside the trade walls. He gave it his blessing and his energies. It allowed him to accept the domestic, economic argument of the anti-Marketeers, while acknowledging British entry as a political fact whose implications the TUC could not ignore.

Within six weeks of the enlargement, Feather's persuasive efforts—in London and the European capitals —were rewarded with his election as the first president of a European Trade Union Confederation. It spoke for the workers' organisations in fifteen countries and represented thirty million members. Heinz Vetter, the West German trade union leader, said that Feather had been elected as an expression of "trust in the British unions vis-à-vis the workers of Europe".

The Conservative victory in the 1970 General Election was a barrage of blows to the TUC. New men were taking

office with a mandate to tame the unions and none of the
Labour Government's fraternal inhibitions. A shift was
promised from collectivism to individualism. Nor could
Victor Feather and the general council absolve themselves
from some responsibility for Harold Wilson's defeat. If
the election was a vote of no confidence in Labour's
economic performance, the failure to carry through the
Government's own industrial relations policy had contributed to the voters' dissatisfaction.

None the less, on the time-honoured principle of the
King is dead, long live the King, the TUC immediately
offered its hand to Edward Heath's administration. The
general council proclaimed its qualified readiness to
co-operate. Its statement should have been stuck, if not on
the new Prime Minister's elegant walls, then certainly on
those of his successive Secretaries of Employment:

"Over the years, consultation between the Government
and both sides of industry has been extended in range and
depth, and the TUC expects of the new Government that
they will maintain this development. The TUC will insist
on its rights to press on the Government policies which it
considers are in the best interests of working people and of
the country as a whole. It will dissent publicly when it
judges that Government proposals are contrary to those
interests, as it has done and will continue to do in opposing
legislative interference in collective bargaining.

"Not only in the field of industrial relations, where their
expert knowledge is most evident, but on all the social and
economic issues which affect the lives of working people,
the TUC general council's judgment will be formed on
merit. Their advice about the way to tackle the social,
economic and industrial problems of this country will be
readily available to this Government, as it was to previous

Governments. The TUC general council expect the Government to recognise the practical and constructive part being played by the trade union movement in the nation's industrial affairs, and the need to retain trade union confidence in the democratic processes of joint consultation."

From the start, the auguries were discouraging. The Conservatives came into a state of whirling inflation and (by recent standards) high unemployment. In Labour's last six months, the unions had been making up for three years of statutory controls. Wage increases of 20 per cent were commonplace, prices followed the trend, and the competitive advantages of the 1967 devaluation were being eroded in foreign markets. 1970 was well on the way to becoming the worst year for strikes since 1926.

Ministers responded with an unblinking severity that was to be their trade mark. Within two months of their election victory, Robert Carr, the Employment Secretary, abandoned the Government's pledge of economic growth and tax cuts. The wage-price spiral, he said, would have to be broken first. After a meeting with the TUC economic committee, Anthony Barber, the new Chancellor of the Exchequer, announced that he was ready to face major strikes in the nationalised industries rather than endorse inflationary pay agreements. In September, Carr refused his Department's conciliation facilities to dustmen and other council workers, unless they agreed in advance to a 14 per cent ceiling to their wage increase. The unions had already rejected this figure. After a frustrating two-hour meeting between the Minister and the unions, Feather saw it as the end of the road for conciliation. "I am afraid that for practical purposes, as far as the unions are concerned, they regard the conciliation function as being not available."

Against this backdrop, the Government presented its plans for the reform of industrial relations. Feather had made a last, forlorn attempt to persuade Robert Carr that an improved voluntary system could do the trick, but on 5 October the Minister published his "consultative document". It contained all the things the unions had feared: a register of trade unions; compulsory and secret ballots; a sixty-day cooling-off period in certain strikes; a National Industrial Relations Court with legislative backing; a strengthened Commission on Industrial Relations with statutory powers; and a ban on the closed shop which can deny work to a man without the right union card.

Feather's reaction was as predictable as the Tory document. The TUC general secretary told a weekend school of colliery officials that all hell would be let loose if people were sent to prison for going on strike. "I think the conduct of this country is so dependent on stable industry and stable relationships that the injection of political conflict into this field is detrimental to the good understanding we need for the growth of our economy and the improvement of living standards." But his answer was still strictly constitutional. "In a democracy," he told a questioner, "you have the right to get people to change their minds, as long as the democratic process operates on a lawful basis."

The "consultative document", though, was not for consultation. The Government's plans were not improvised. They were the fruit of long gestation in opposition. Carr informed the TUC that there could be no bargaining about matters of substance, only on details. The Minister refused to extend the period for discussion beyond 13 November, one month away. There was, in other words, to be no Second Battle of Downing Street. The general council responded with a boycott of future talks with the

Government until Ministers agreed to broaden them beyond questions of detail. "If there is no response from Mr Carr," Feather said, "then future talks would be like a dialogue of the deaf."

Did the TUC have any choice? Could the general secretary have tried to lead in any other direction? Tom Jackson, of the Union of Post Office Workers, argued at this meeting of the general council that they had to negotiate with the Government. That was what they were good at. How often had they been confronted with employers who said the unions had heard their last word? And how often had they still wrung concessions from them? The argument was taken up by Jack Peel, the Yorkshire textile workers' leader, but neither he nor Jackson had the weight or seniority to command attention. On the Left of the general council, Jack Jones and Hugh Scanlon were feeling their strength. They were committed ideologically to Shop Steward Power. They were ready for a fight. Although the Right-wing general councillors had no more taste than the Left for "anti-trade union legislation", they might in other circumstances have supported negotiation as a practical last resort. They were checked, however, by the memory of June 1969. Having humbled their own Labour Government so recently on the same battlefield, they owed a fight to Harold Wilson. In the shadow of the Conservative election victory, Feather shared these reservations. His fixer's instincts were suppressed. Instead, the general secretary threw his energies into a campaign against the Tory Bill that was to cost the TUC £120,000 and the movement as a whole about £250,000.

Conservative Ministers were surprised at the degree of sustained hostility their proposals provoked. While they were still in opposition, Robert Carr and his industrial relations team had met privately over the lunch table with several union leaders. Their impression was that, for all the initial outcry, the unions would come to terms with the Bill. Some union leaders had even shown themselves happier with the Tory proposals, which at least lodged the penal powers with a court, than with Barbara Castle's, which had wanted to give them to a politician. Like their Labour precursors, the Conservatives hoped, too, that the unions would eventually be prepared to buy the positive proposals—the statutory right to union membership, compensation for unfair dismissal, and the limited right of access by the unions to company books relevant to collective bargaining. They probably overestimated the congeniality of their guests. In any case, the Conservatives' other economic policies made co-operation less palatable than ever.

Growth, so early abandoned, was a cornerstone of all the TUC's economic thinking. It would provide jobs. It would make it possible for employers to pay higher wages in return for higher productivity. A rational voluntary incomes policy would be acceptable. Instead, the Government opted for a limited, discriminatory restraint. It tried to use its power as an employer and paymaster to slow the pace for industry as a whole. To the unions—and to much of public opinion—this looked like hitting the weak to teach the strong a lesson. It was doubly insufferable from a Government that preached self-sufficiency and competition; that refused to countenance any formal restriction on prices and dividends; and that seemed unable to stop unemployment climbing steadily from 500,000 to 1,000,000.

The one union leader of the Right—big, thick-skinned and combative enough to have resisted the triumph of what George Woodcock used to call the "non-co-operators"—was Les Cannon. But the electricians' president was missing from the general council, suffering from the cancer that killed him at the age of fifty on 9 December. Like his successor, Frank Chapple, two years later, Cannon would probably have fought for negotiation rather than boycott. He might have been a rallying point for those who shared Tom Jackson's misgivings, but the chances would still have been slight.

The Conservative Industrial Relations Bill was published on 3 December 1970. Its draft code of industrial practice followed six months later. By September 1971, after a clause-by-clause struggle through Parliament, the Act was on the Statute Book. In the interval, Feather was seldom off the front pages. In January, he shared an Albert Hall platform with Harold Wilson and Citrine at the climax of a "Day of Protest" against the Bill. It turned, as it happened, into an evening of protest by the ultra Left against the orthodox leadership of the Labour Party and the TUC. In February, he led a march of anything from 125,000 to 150,000 trade unionists from Hyde Park to Trafalgar Square. They came to London in 230 buses, thirty-eight special trains and two aircraft. The march stretched for seven miles and was enlivened by twenty-three brass and pipe bands.

"This," Feather exulted from the plinth of Nelson's Column, "is D-Day, 1971. D for demonstration. D for democracy. . . . The lame ducks in this country are in the Cabinet, limping about on thin ice and quacking away about uniting the nation." (John Davies, the Conservative Secretary for Trade and Industry, must by now have regretted his choice of imagery, if not his policy of leaving inefficient companies to perish.)

Feather was in his element. The TUC was going out to

Receiving an honorary degree from Harold Wilson at Bradford
University, December 1970

Garland

"TED! THERE COMES A TIME WHEN A MAN'S GOTTA DO WHAT A MAN'S GOTTA DO!"

Cartoon by Garland dated 22 February 1972

the workers, and the workers were responding by the thousand. The Trafalgar Square demonstration, which spilled over into Temple Gardens, was as impressive for its discipline as for its numbers. These were no wild, habitual protesters. Later, Feather also marched in demonstrations against unemployment; in regional protests against the Bill; and in support of the workers at Upper Clyde Shipbuilders, who refused to take bankruptcy for an answer and finally shamed the Government into finding them a buyer who could preserve their jobs. The rational motive was always the same: Feather was taking the TUC into the branch room. He was careful, however, to draw a line between democratic pressure and revolution. A Trotskyist intellectual hailed the Upper Clyde work-in as the beginning of a thousand-year march. Feather followed him on the same radio news magazine, and quickly insisted that the shipbuilders were "working themselves into a job, not into the history books".

At the same time, Feather was establishing himself as conciliator-in-chief to the nation. The Department of Employment, heir to the shrewd and pliant Ministry of Labour, had lost the political will to make industrial peace. Increasingly, too, it was losing the experienced manpower to do the job. The unions had also abandoned their faith in arbitration since the Conservatives had taken to using it as an instrument of Government policy. Feather was a willing and skilled alternative. Sometimes, as in the postmen's strike or the power workers' strike in the winter of 1970–71, he jerked the Government into intervening. Sometimes, as with the miners' dispute a year later, he brought the two sides together. Sometimes, as with the national newspaper industry, the employers turned to Feather for conciliation and were glad to go to

N

Congress House for it. His technique was subtle and flexible: good advance staff work on the telephone; a minimum of protocol; the patience to flit from room to room, whittling the points of conflict. "Why insist on a categorical undertaking?" he asked one set of employers. "An ordinary undertaking is good enough. Don't screw the balls off the boys. They have to sell it to the lads." The rôle was highly personal. The fact that Feather was general secretary of the TUC gave him the authority to carry his conciliation through, but it is not necessarily something you can pass on to a successor. At this level, it is not likely to stay a permanent part of the TUC's function.

Throughout the twenty-two months that Robert Carr was Employment Secretary, his working relationship with Feather stayed cold and distant. This was out of character both for his Department and for the Minister. The tradition of the former Ministry of Labour was the tradition of British industrial relations professionals: pragmatic, informal, accessible, a private world in which enemies called each other by their first names and knew each other's telephone numbers. Conservative Ministers of Labour—even the steely Edward Heath—had reigned in the spirit of the club. By reputation and temperament, Carr was assumed to be out of the same mould as Walter Monckton, the urbane peacemaker of the fifties. He was genial and softly-spoken. He had worked once as a night foreman (in the family firm). He was supposed to know what industry was about.

While Carr was Shadow Minister, Feather had respected him as a fellow practitioner. What the unions had underestimated was Carr's very Conservative commitment to the ideal of order, in industry as in society at large, and the uncompromising style that Heath stamped on his administration. Once the TUC had rejected consultation on Government terms, Carr and Feather met privately no more than two or three times, and none of these meetings was productive. The longest was a lunch at the Garrick Club. A well-meaning knight, who happened to know the Minister and the general secretary, felt it was a shame that two good chaps couldn't get together, patch up their differences over the claret, and lead this island to prosperity. Feather saw little point, but hadn't the heart to refuse the invitation. The pair restated their positions. Carr had to get back to the House of Commons, Feather to the TUC. Both were grateful for an excuse to part. The dialogue was still of the deaf.

The Conservative strategy was designed to bring discipline into relations between workers and employers, and to put the economy on a stable footing. Within two years it had failed in both objectives. Industrial Britain often looked like Sauchiehall Street on a Saturday night. State of emergency followed state of emergency. Stinking refuse spilled on to the unswept pavements. The nation shivered in the candlelight, factories and offices went on short time for want of power and heating. The mail and the railways were halted. Picketing turned to violence. The National Industrial Relations Court committed five London dockers to Pentonville; fined the Transport and General Workers £55,000; and made an ass of itself, the law and Victor Feather. The Cabinet stunned, then revived, its two most flamboyant lame ducks, Upper Clyde Shipbuilders and Rolls-Royce. In June 1972, only two years after Roy Jenkins had left the Tories the biggest balance of payments surplus in history, the pound was allowed to float, a thinly camouflaged devaluation. By the end of the year, Heath was turning to statutory control of prices and incomes, against which he had set his face ever since taking office.

It was, however, a sour vindication for the TUC and its general secretary. Unemployment remained stubbornly high, the economy stagnant, and exports shaky. The limits as well as the strengths of union solidarity were exposed. The posturings of Trafalgar Square undermined Feather's efforts to lead the TUC back into Whitehall. In the running fight with the Conservative Government, he could never recapture the personal authority or the general council unanimity of the Battle of Labour Downing Street. The Left-wing union leaders set the pace. Even when they were defeated—as over Hugh Scanlon's demand at the 1972 congress for a total boycott of the Industrial Relations Act and all its works—they dictated the terms of the debate. A qualified boycott was hailed as a victory for the "moderates", yet the same Brighton assembly brusquely suspended thirty-two member unions, representing nearly 500,000 workers, for refusing to withdraw from the Government's register of trade unions. Nor were the Left-wing leaders always free to choose their battlefields. Jack Jones was hoist with his own doctrine of devolution, and on one occasion was jostled and hectored by militant dockers.

The campaign on the wages front did not go all one way. Jack Scamp, an arbitrator of the old school, breached the Government limit by awarding the "dirty jobs" men 15 per cent in November 1970. Lord Wilberforce followed with a more ambiguous package for the power station workers (11 per cent or 16 per cent, depending on whose statistician you listened to). But the postal strike was a clear defeat—for Tom Jackson, the postmen's general secretary, and for the TUC that had cheered him into the trenches. The stoppage lasted forty-seven days, the longest national strike in history, but ended with a 9 per cent pay increase. The Union of Post Office Workers was divided. Its members in the telephone and Telex services went on working in sufficient numbers to blunt the effect on business and government. The union lacked the necessary funds to sustain a long strike. Ironically, workshop collections were hampered by the absence of postal services. But, critically for Jackson, other unions would not finance his stoppage. They would lend him money, but not give it. Jackson told the TUC general council that he would need £250,000 a week to keep the strike going. He was offered another loan, of £50,000 by the Amalgamated Engineers. The choice was between settling with the Post Office, or burdening his union with the sort of debt it would never be able to repay. Jackson settled.

From the postmen's humiliation in May 1971, to the end of the year, the Government seemed gradually to be winning. Wage rises in the public sector stayed relatively low. In February 1972, the power workers (back in the queue) were content to accept 7¾ per cent. But the miners soon stilled any celebrations in the Carlton Club.

The miners had not been on strike since the General Strike and its sequel in 1926. They felt a deep sense of grievance. Over the previous decade, under the wise guidance of Will Paynter, they had co-operated in running down the industry from 700,000 men to fewer than 300,000 with parallel increases in productivity. Yet their earnings had fallen behind those of workers in manufacturing industry. They insisted that they were a special case, and most of the public agreed. Their strike lasted more than seven weeks (another new record) and won them pay rises of more than 20 per cent. The secret of their resounding success was first that it was solid. The mining villages form tight communities with a long folk-lore of hardship and struggle. Although their union paid no strike benefit, the miners stayed away. Secondly, their picketing not only stopped work in the mines but blockaded the power stations. The miners persuaded lorry drivers to stop delivering coal already mined and paid for. Almost by accident, they discovered at the same time that they could turn back supplies of oil and chemicals needed for firing the generating plants.

It was lucky for the Establishment that the miners were not a revolutionary breed. Their strike demonstrated just how quickly the economy could be brought to its knees. Picketing was ruthless and sometimes illegal, but most chief constables drew back from prosecuting thousands of angry and organised men. Other unions instructed their members not to cross picket lines, but otherwise left the fight to the miners. Feather flew back prematurely from Miami Beach, where he had been persuading American port and airport workers not to black British cargoes in protest at the shooting of Roman Catholics in Northern Ireland. His first instinct was to leave the Government to pull its own chestnuts from the fire, but eventually he brought the miners' leaders, Joe Gormley and Lawrence Daly, together with the National Coal Board. Lord Wilberforce's mediation produced an offer of 20 per cent, which the miners increased with one final turn of the screw before going back to the pits. 'N-minus one', the Government's policy of forcing wage settlements down one step at a time, was dead.

The Industrial Relations Act came into operation by

stages like a slow fuse. The first effects of the union boycott were felt by the Commission on Industrial Relations,
the benevolent uncle established to promote voluntary
reform. George Woodcock resigned as its chairman as
early as March 1971. Alf Allen and Will Paynter, the
two part-time trade union members, had already withdrawn. By the autumn, the commission's annual report
complained that the TUC boycott was hampering its work.

The first confrontation between the unions and the
Industrial Relations Court came in March 1972. Liverpool dockers had been ordered to stop blacking container
lorries belonging to Heatons Transport of St Helens. The
shop stewards had ignored the order. The court, therefore, fined their union, the Transport and General
Workers, £5,000. The union had not put in an appearance. The Heatons dispute was precisely the kind of
situation the unions had warned Labour and Conservative
Governments about. The dockers were anxious for their
jobs. Over the previous four years their industry had
shrunk rapidly. Now they were threatened with a further
decline because hauliers were packing containers at their
own depots, and incidentally with cheaper labour. Because
their complaints had not been answered, the dockers took
to industrial action. They refused to allow the containers
into the docks. The problem was not restricted to the
Mersey. It had to be resolved comprehensively between
unions and employers. Feather was quick to point
the moral: "Swingeing fines on unions will not force
British workers to modify their objections to the
Industrial Relations Act. Punitive actions do not help
to resolve disputes between employers and workers.
The Government must by now be regretting that it
started the process in which unnecessary legislation

hinders useful dialogue with both sides of industry."

Jack Jones stuck to TUC policy, refusing either to pay the fine or to communicate with the court. In April the court replied by adding £50,000 to the transport union's penalty. For once, Feather's gift for public relations seemed to desert him. "Everybody learns by experience," he said in a television interview. "I think to some degree that this court was thought to be similar to a tribunal. I have now learned that it is a court in the same class and character as the Old Bailey." As the industrial writers briskly reminded him, this was exactly what they—and no doubt Feather's legal advisers—had been telling him for months.

The general secretary's delusion was not, however, without some foundation. The court's president, Sir John Donaldson, had made much play of its lack of judicial pomp. He was a judge, but his two colleagues were laymen with experience of industrial relations. They sat in lounge suits. Donaldson was approachable by the specialist press in a way more reminiscent of Jack Scamp than of the Lord Chief Justice. But as the law set out as clearly as a bell, the National Industrial Relations Court had the status of a High Court. To flaunt its rulings was to flaunt the law. Sir John underlined the argument with a brief lecture in elementary jurisprudence:

"Without the rule of law and courts to enforce it, each one of us would be free to push and bully our fellow citizens and, which may be thought more important, our fellow citizens would be free to push and bully us. In a free-for-all none of us could hope to be the winner. The justification for law, the courts and the rule of law is that they protect us from unfair and oppressive actions by others. But if we are to have the protection, we must ourselves accept that the law applies to us too and limits our freedom. In civilised countries nearly everyone accepts this and agrees that it is a small price to pay. There remain the few who want to use the laws which suit them and disobey those which do not. If the rule of law is to have any meaning, the courts must in the last resort take action against these few and impose some penalty."

The first response to Feather's pronouncement was of incredulity. In the Department of Employment, however, it was read as a smoke signal from Congress House. The TUC had abandoned its extra-legal campaign against the Act. It was time to change course, and the general secretary was letting both the Government and his members know it. If Ministers assumed that the unions would now trip like lambs through Donaldson's door, they were more than premature. But the £55,000 fines concentrated the trade union mind. The general council drew up guidelines for unions threatened before the court. The right of self-defence was acknowledged. As Feather put it: "We don't see any bonus in being hit and leaving ourselves defenceless. The bloody elephant is still there, even if you turn your back on it. And, meanwhile, it is expensive to feed it with peanuts at £50,000 a time."

At the court's next hearing the Transport and General Workers were represented by counsel. The TUC advised Jack Jones to pay. The union agreed, but insisted that congress should foot the bill. It was, after all, the TUC boycott that had caused the trouble. The general council recognised "moral responsibility" for some of the fine, and eventually it paid about £20,000 of the union's costs. The issue was shelved in June when the Court of Appeal set aside the fines on the ground that a union was not responsible for the acts of its shop stewards, but this in turn was reversed by the House of Lords in July.

By then the drama had switched from the Mersey to the Thames, and the spectre of trade unionists behind bars had become a reality. Three stewards in the London docks were ordered to prison for ignoring an Industrial Relations Court instruction to stop picketing lorries from the Chobham Farm terminal. The original dispute was similar to that at Heatons. Should containers be packed by registered dockers or by hauliers' men? The three stewards, Bernie Steer, Vic Turner and Alan Williams, were threatening not only to continue picketing, but to spread the blacking of lorries. Steer, a Communist who had been a docker for twelve years, greeted the committal order with deliberate defiance: "All three of us will not co-operate with the Industrial Relations Court. We do not recognise the court and will have no dealings with it. I am not pleased about the thought of going to prison, but if that is what our struggle means, we will certainly go." Dockers in Britain's two major ports, London and Liverpool, immediately announced that they would strike in support of the three stewards.

The Government, the Labour correspondents reported, was "bewildered". The case had been brought against the dockers by workers at the Chobham Farm terminal. The Government was not a party, but would have to sweep up the pieces after the law had taken its course. Instead, by a welcome theatrical coup the Court of Appeal set aside the committal order. The evidence of contempt, according to Lord Denning, Master of the Rolls, was unsatisfactory. The genie of the lamp was Norman Turner, the Official Solicitor, a public servant few people had even heard of before. One of his tasks was to see that citizens sent to prison for contempt were not left to rot. Turner briefed Peter Pain, the Transport and General's QC, without asking the dockers. Denning's decision undermined the authority of the Industrial Relations Court and made a laughing stock of the Act. Within a week, the Chobham Farm dispute was resolved by conventional means. The management and the union, which represented the workers on both sides of the conflict, agreed that the terminal would in future be manned by registered dockers, forty of whom would be taken on immediately. The sixty-three non-dockers already working at Chobham Farm would not be dismissed.

The dock stewards did not, however, have to wait long for their bread and water. The new militancy soon secured its martyrs. Early in July the Industrial Relations Court ordered dockers to stop blacking vehicles using the Midland Cold Storage Company's depot in Stratford, East London. The dispute was again about who should load lorries. On 21 July 1972, the court ordered five dockers—Bernie Steer, Vic Turner, Derek Watkins, Cornelius Clancy and Anthony Merrick—to be jailed for contempt. "The issue," Sir John Donaldson said, "is whether these men are allowed to opt out of the rule of law. Can they pick and choose, relying on it for the protection of their homes and families but rejecting it when, even temporarily, it obstructs their industrial objectives? It is a very simple issue, but vastly important, for our whole way of life is based upon the acceptance of the rule of law." The High Court tipstaff, James Dorling, went by taxi to the East End and read the five names on his warrant to a picket line. Watkins, Clancy and Merrick stepped forward and were taken in a police van to Pentonville. Steer and Turner soon joined them in the prison.

Caught between the rule of law and the sort of unofficial action he had always resisted, Feather could do no more than sing his familiar tune. The damage that the Act was doing to the nation was now clear to everybody, he said. Putting people in prison solved nothing. It made an already difficult situation even more difficult to resolve. The immediate effect of the dockers' imprisonment was a walkout by 170,000 workers. The *Observer* called it the "most significant challenge to the authority of any Government since the General Strike of 1926". The ports and newspapers were shut down. Miners stopped work in Yorkshire, Scotland and Wales. In the capital busmen, airport staff and porters at the Covent Garden and Smithfield markets went on strike. The TUC called (but later withdrew) a national twenty-four-hour stoppage.

After five days the "Pentonville Five" were released, once more after the intervention of the Official Solicitor. "He is not," Sir John Donaldson said, "a political or industrial fairy godmother armed with a magic key which unlocks prisons." In fact, the lock had been turned by the Law Lords, who had ruled earlier the same day that unions were responsible for the action of their stewards. On that assumption, the Industrial Relations Court was content that the dockers had purged their contempt. Passions took longer to cool in the docks. A delegate meeting threw out a container-handling agreement devised after months of deliberation by a committee under the joint chairmanship of Jack Jones and Lord Aldington, chairman of the Port of London Authority and a former deputy chairman of the Conservative Party. Jones and Aldington had to go back to the drawing board, while 42,000 dockers went on indefinite strike.

The case of the Pentonville Five taught the Cabinet just how much tinder it was playing with. Significantly, Ministers did not dream of invoking another of the main props of the Industrial Relations Act to delay the dock strike. There was no question of a cooling-off period or a compulsory ballot. The lesson of the railway dispute earlier that summer had been learned. The railwaymen voted six-to-one against a 12·5 per cent pay offer. Although the Government was "determined" not to allow any further increase, agreement was eventually sealed at 13·5 per cent,

The Industrial Relations Act nevertheless remained on the Statute Book. Jack Jones had to pay his £55,000, and Hugh Scanlon's Engineers another £55,000 for barring a member from branch meetings. And the TUC had to discipline its own recalcitrants, the thirty-two unions that had refused to withdraw from the register. For Victor Feather, the Brighton congress was painful and difficult. Only a year earlier, the TUC under his leadership had broken the barrier of 10,000,000 affiliated members. But now the general secretary recognised the inevitability of suspension. Majorities, he said, had their rights too. It was the kind of attacking stroke Feather often plays when he knows he is on a bad wicket. His main concern was to keep down the temperature. There must be no denunciations, no bell, book and candle. If that meant dictatorial control from the chair, so be it. An angry, emotional confrontation would leave deeper wounds.

Within these uneasy terms of reference, Feather's tactics succeeded. The gate was left open for the thirty-two unions to remove themselves from the register and return to the fold before the next congress. The alternative would be expulsion. Feather's speech on behalf of the general council balanced firmness and tact: "The unions have a long association with congress, and let us acknowledge the contribution they have made. And let us hope that well before this year is out these unions—every single one of them—will follow the overwhelming majority and make it possible for their suspension to be lifted."

Most of the thirty-two were tiny craft unions—like the National Union of Scalemakers, the Coopers' Federation, the Funeral Service Operatives and the National Union of Basket, Cane, Wicker and Fibre Furniture Makers of Great Britain and Ireland—backed by the jet-setting, but still relatively small, Professional Footballers and Trainers, Actors' Equity and the British Airline Pilots' Association. The list did, however, include three major unions—the printing craftsmen of the National Graphical Association, the Confederation of Health Service Employees, and the National Union of Seamen—as well as the National Union of Bank Employees, an expanding white-collar union that had won a glorious fight for recognition in the late sixties. The argument running through the speeches on behalf of the ten unions that chose to defend themselves before congress was that some unions (notably the Seamen, Equity and the Bank Employees) had special problems of recruitment, control or competition from staff associations that could be resolved only by staying on the register. This would give them the right to seek a legally-enforced closed shop, one of the few concessions wrung from the Government during the Industrial Relations Bill's passage through Parliament. Few of the thirty-two opted for Feather's way back anything like so quickly as the general secretary had hoped.

The night the miners' strike ended, 27 February 1972, Edward Heath broadcast to the nation. "We have," the Prime Minister said, "to find a more sensible way of settling our differences." Six months earlier four men had come to the same unoriginal conclusion. Victor Feather of the TUC, Campbell Adamson, director-general of the

Confederation of British Industry, Sir Douglas Allen, Permanent Secretary of the Treasury, and Sir Frank Figgures, director-general of the National Economic Development Office, began meeting at fortnightly intervals. They came alone. No other officials were present when they discussed the economy and prepared the ground for the monthly sessions of the National Economic Development Council, the planning forum which brings together Government, unions and industry. They could say what they liked. Their words did not have to be tailored to their constituents. In July 1972, the "Group of Four" became the "Group of Five". Sir William Armstrong, the head of the Home Civil Service, began attending its meetings. Armstrong, the most powerful man in Whitehall, was there as the eyes and ears of Edward Heath. The group, which had been a valued channel of communication, became central to the Government's search for "a more sensible way", not only of avoiding strikes but of managing the economy.

Diplomatic relations had been resumed meanwhile between Congress House and Downing Street. Overtures began in December 1971, when the TUC general council was invited to No. 10. The Prime Minister went out of his way to emphasise that he wanted to do business with the TUC. Feather's response at that stage was guarded: "The Government would, I think, like to have a closer dialogue. So would I, but not simply a dialogue of acceptance of preconceived Government doctrines that have not worked too well so far." Ambassadors were exchanged on 9 March, only ten days after the miners' stoppage. The TUC went again to Downing Street and had its best meeting in twenty months with Conservative economic Ministers. The Employment Secretary, Robert

Carr, said afterwards: "We have to seek the common ground which exists between us and work on it and build on it for the good of the whole country." Feather, echoing his own December statement, said: "We have heard enough to encourage further dialogue. It was a good meeting and useful." Another union leader said privately: "For the first time the Government was almost pleading with us for help and seemed ready to pay the price."

A month later, Heath reshuffled his Cabinet. Carr became Leader of the Commons, replacing William Whitelaw, the new Secretary for Northern Ireland. Maurice Macmillan went to St James's Square as Employment Secretary. After an awkward start, with Macmillan trying to be as abrasive as his master, the change helped to clear the air. Although there was still none of the old intimacy between the TUC and the Minister, contact was more relaxed. Feather still did not ask for meetings, but when Macmillan invited him for a private chat the general secretary went. Such encounters remained irregular, but they became more frequent. It was not a question of personality. The situation had changed. Macmillan's brief was different from Carr's, and he was not tarred for trade unionists as the man who had grappled the Industrial Relations Act into law. But the focus, for industrial relations and for the economy, had moved from St James's Square across the park to Downing Street.

On 12 July the TUC agreed to join the Government and the CBI in "talks about talks". The unions insisted, however, that these be conducted through the machinery of the National Economic Development Council. This was not so much a snub to the Prime Minister, who had invited the TUC to join Ministers in a special working party, as a device for ensuring that the unions would be

Cartoon by John Kent dated 21 August 1972

Vic Feather as general secretary

represented by a strong and balanced team. There was still an emotional resistance to co-operation, both in the general council and among rank-and-file trade unionists. The London docks container dispute was still on the boil. The pit and railway strikes were fresh in the memory. But the TUC had not withdrawn from the development council, and there was no reason why its six-man delegation should not extend participation into meetings with the Government and industry. The six were Victor Feather, Hugh Scanlon, Jack Jones, Lord Cooper of the General and Municipal Workers, Sidney Greene of the Railwaymen, and Alfred Allen of the Shopworkers. The two Left-wingers, Scanlon and Jones, would have found it hard to explain their attendance to their militant members. Without them, the talks would have been pointless.

For Feather the incentive was twofold. In the last resort, the unions could not choose the Government. They had to work for the benefit of their members, with whichever Administration the voters elected. Boycott was neither the general secretary's style, nor the TUC's interest. And, more immediately, inflation was mocking the unions' struggle. What use were wage increases if prices soared? The result was the most important sequence of discussions between Government and union leaders since June 1969. Ten sessions, at Chequers and in Downing Street, stretched from July to November. In the end they failed. This time there were no winners.

Feather staked everything on a voluntary agreement to control wages and prices. Through Sir William Armstrong, the general secretary convinced Heath that the TUC might be able to deliver the goods. The ideas presented by the Government had originated in Congress House: a flat-rate monetary increase (in the Heath

o

version £2 a week) for everyone, rather than percentage limits which meant more to managing directors than to their lift men; a threshold agreement, under which a rise would be triggered automatically if the cost of living went up by more than, say, 6 per cent; higher pensions; and a commitment to a 5 per cent annual growth of the economy.

On at least half a dozen occasions during the four months of negotiation, Feather went secretly to Downing Street for private meetings with the Prime Minister. Sometimes the two men sat down alone, more often Sir William Armstrong was there too. These were not negotiating sessions. As with similar visits during the conflict with Harold Wilson, Feather was trying to guide the Prime Minister's hand to what would be acceptable. Heath asked questions, Feather offered answers, Armstrong listened. Feather came away satisfied that Heath wanted to reach an agreement.

Why, then, did the negotiations fail? The most persuasive verdict was delivered by Eric Jacobs in a *Sunday Times* inquest on 5 November, three days after the talks were pronounced dead:

"There were some things the Government did not consider it could discuss with the unions because they were matters for decision by Government and Parliament alone. . . . Mr Heath had indeed been at pains to point out that, though the effects of the policies could be discussed, the policies themselves could not, and among these he listed entry to Europe, the Housing Finance Act, the Industrial Relations Act and taxation. The Government, in other words, would negotiate, but it would not abdicate. And the trade unionists disliked so much of the Government's previous record that—taken together with their reservations about particular items in the package and the proposed loss of their individual negotiating freedom—they could not in the last resort bring themselves to accept Mr Heath's offer."

John Elliott took a crisper line in the *Financial Times* a day earlier. "The Prime Minister and the TUC," he wrote, "had two completely different views of what they were doing in Downing Street. The TUC thought they were negotiating, the Prime Minister only that they were discussing an economic package." Elliott's interpretation draws sustenance from Heath's own comment after the breakdown: "We always emphasised that these talks were not carried on as a bargaining session. They were carried on in an endeavour to find a rational way of handling these economic problems and try to get people to agree upon the figures."

Victor Feather's considered conclusion is that the distinction between "negotiation" and "getting people to agree upon the figures" is synthetic. To any trade union leader, agreement on figures which their members will accept can come only through negotiation. Otherwise, you are back to the acceptance of preconceived Government doctrines.

"On 26 September", Feather says, "the Government put forward their proposals. Everybody had been talking, particularly the Government, about reaching a collective agreement. They'd been talking about a partnership. They'd been talking about a social contract. Where there is an agreement, or a partnership, or a contract, that involves two parties. So, therefore, on 10 October we put forward our counter-proposals. We'd been talking about negotiations. Even as early as July, the checklist had included the Industrial Relations Act, pensions, the Common Market and the Housing Finance Act—all the

o*

various factors that enter into prices and the standard of living. We put our counter-proposals forward on 10 October. These had been discussed, and then we were all very surprised and disappointed when, right at the end, the Prime Minister came out with the view that certain things could not be included in the negotiations.

"The talks broke down because we were all disappointed. It seemed to us that on 26 September (and in the talks previously and in the talks later) that we were making progress. We went to a great deal of trouble, a lot of hours, working parties, working groups. We cancelled engagements all over the place in order to fit in these talks, and we wanted them to succeed. That goes for all of us, completely unanimous. And then when the Prime Minister came up with his statement on 2 November, his final statement, we looked at it and said it wasn't a basis for negotiation."

This was partly because the Government was putting up "Out of bounds" notices in too many places the unions thought significant, but more especially because they felt the restraint on prices was going to be less effective than that on wages. Feather and his posse of compulsive bargainers demanded a freeze on all prices, although most of them knew this was impossible. They shifted to talking about the weekly shopping basket, and later to seeking an "undertaking" about the dozen basic foodstuffs. Now it was the Government's turn to talk about distinctions without a difference. If Ministers gave an undertaking to keep down food prices, they would have to put it through Parliament. But they could not legislate for prices without legislating for wages. The unions must accept both or neither.

Ultimately, the division was not between two habits of

mind or two modes of life. It was a division between men answerable to different constituencies. For trade unionists, the conflicts of the thirty Tory months followed four years of strain, battle and disenchantment with a Labour Government. This time it was the TUC that needed copper-bottomed guarantees. Without a convincing assurance on prices, Feather could not commit the general council and the union leaders could not commit their members. No Downing Street treaty could promise peace for our industrial time. On the Government side, Heath was constantly aware of Conservative backbench opinion. It is always easier to lead your troops up the hill to war than down to compromise. The bracing strategy of cold baths and self-sufficiency had failed, but Heath had to calculate every inch of his way back. How much would they tolerate, the Enoch Powells and Angus Maudes, and all the stout Tories beside them? Parliament, the Prime Minister told the unions on 30 October, would not accept statutory price controls with no equivalent for incomes. For "Parliament", read "the Conservative benches".

On 2 November the talks broke down. Edward Heath invited the leaders of unions and industry to a cold buffet supper. They ate and dispersed. On the following Monday, 6 November, the Prime Minister announced to an unsurprised House of Commons that prices and wages would be frozen. "We have come to the conclusion that we have no alternative but to bring in statutory measures to secure these agreed objectives of economic management in the light of the proposals discussed in the tripartite talks." The unions returned to Trafalgar Square. Strike followed work-to-rule; a May Day of protest followed another special congress. The tragedy was not only Victor Feather's.

Index

by

H. E. CROWE

Developing countries, VF's work
for unions in 89
Diary of VF typical week 182–3
Diplomacy of 18, 19, 20
Disputes, TUC statistics 172–3
Dockers, court of appeal for 203
gaoled 195, 200, 203
strike in support of 204
Doctor of Technology 38
Donaldson, Sir John, National
Industrial Relations Court
president 200–1, 203–4
Donovan Commission on trade
unions and employers' associa-
tions 130–1, 134, 143, 169,
175
Dorling, James, High Court tip-
staff 204
Douglas-Home, Alec 18
Downing Street, No. 10, meetings
74, 130, 137, 142, 143, 144,
146, 147, 155, 171, 174, 208,
210
Downing Street Declaration 160,
161
Drogheda Committee 90
Dukes, Charlie 87
Dunnett, Sir James 130

EAM (Greek National Front of
Liberation) 76
Economic League 45
Eden, Anthony, Foreign Secretary
69, 74
Election agent for East Ward,
Bradford 44
Electrical Trades Union (ETU)
35, 96, 107, 108
ballot-rigging of 103–4
campaign against 15
Communist control of 102–4
expulsion from TUC 96, 104
Elizabeth II, Queen, at TUC
celebrations 118
Engineering Union (AEU, later
AEF, later AUEW) 151,
152, 153, 155, 190, 196, 197,
205, 209
European Economic Community,
problem of 186
European Free Trade Association
186
European Trade Union Confederation, VF first president of
186

Fair Deal at Work, Conservative
Party programme 132
Fascists 66
Feather, Alice, wife of VF 60, 64,
65, 183
Feather, Edith Mabel, mother 17,
23, 31, 32, 33, 39–42
Feather, Edwin, brother 12, 15,
21, 28, 38
Feather, Harry, father 13, 14, 21,
22, 23, 28, 29, 43
and conscientious objectors 30
death of 38
family of 12, 13, 15, 21–7
at Gainsborough 28, 34
stroke 37–42
union worker 29
war work 29
Feather, Jack Hyndman, brother
21
Feather, Pat, daughter 61, 64
Feather, Sandy, son 61, 124
FEATHER, VICTOR GRAYSON
HARDIE:
accident and illness 30–1
christened 32
early days 20–7, 39, 40
education 15, 16, 26, 34–6, 44,
46, 67
family of 60, 61, 64, 124
married 60–1
progress in TUC 16, 64, 91,
110 ff., 167
See also Trades Union Congress
and entries throughout the
index for further details